How to Plan and Develop a Career Center

by Don Schutt

Ferguson Publishing Company
Chicago, Illinois

Acknowledgements

The editor would like to extend his thanks to Roger Lambert at the Center on Education and Work for his insights and assistance on this project and to Joyce Thompson, also at the Center on Education and Work, for her administrative assistance with the book. Special thanks go to Paul Phifer, Director of the Career Resource and Assessment Center at Grand Rapids Community College, for his helpful commentary on the original manuscript.

Contributing Authors

Steve Bialek, Shelley Drescher, Judith Ettinger, Pamela Hilleshiem-Setz, Carl McDaniels, Kathleen Schaefers, April Schnell, Eric Schnell, and Barb Taylor

How to plan and develop a career center.
        p. cm.
        ISBN 0-89434-241-X
        1. Career edcation--Information services--United States--Planning. 2. Vocational guidance--Information services--United States--Planning. I. J.G. Ferguson Publishing Company.
LC1037.5.H667   1999
370.11.'3'0973--dc21   98-35598
                                         CIP

Copyright ©1999 Ferguson Publishing Company.
Published and Distributed by
Ferguson Publishing Company
200 West Madison Street, Suite 300
Chicago, IL 60606
312-580-5480
www.fergpubco.com

Printed in the United States of America.   V-10

Table of Contents

Introduction

by Don Schutt

Not so long ago, career centers focused almost exclusively on matching people to jobs—the so-called "trait and factor" approach. Clients' aptitudes and abilities were assessed, generally at the high school level, the results of those assessments then being used to inform clients of the "right" job or the "right" post-secondary education for them. Direct placement services were sometimes offered but, as often as not, clients were left to find employment through family contacts or the classified ads.

Within this narrow range of goals, these old career centers frequently met with success. As the world of work began to change, however, career centers based on the trait and factor approach became less able to serve their clients effectively. As is discussed in depth in Chapter One, as the world of work shifted from an industrial society to one driven by information and technology, thus began the demise of the paternalistic employer who looked after his employees their entire working life—as well as the demise of the employee willing to settle for stability in lieu of greater challenge and fulfillment. At the same time, educational and training opportunities were expanding: access to universities increased for women, racial and ethnic minorities, and the less affluent; vocational courses at technical schools opened doors for those previously shut out of the old apprenticeship and on-the-job training systems. Career centers still operating on the notion that one person in one job equals a career could hardly hope for success in such a world.

Yet further changes await even those centers that tried to adapt to the broadened definition of *career* as a lifetime of growth and achievement instead of a solitary job and to accept the expanded horizons of every person inhabiting the world of work. Today's

1

workplace must address the new concerns of diversity, downsizing, lifelong learning, and the astonishing progress of technology. Whether they serve second graders or senior citizens, assembly line workers or academic researchers, career centers must take all of these factors into account and provide services geared toward today's world of work—and ready for tomorrow's.

Many of you might think this is easier said than done, but as with most challenging problems, things become less complicated when the main task of career centers is broken down into its components. According to the National Career Development Association (NCDA), career centers can meet the needs of both adults and youth in the community by providing:

- extensive self-appraisal, using a wide variety of instruments related to lifelong career development;
- extensive career information, including local, state, and national data concerning a wide variety of occupations as well as the education/training needed for each;
- career counseling services conducted by qualified professionals;
- career training facilities designed to help persons acquire necessary skills for finding and keeping a job, making career decisions, and identifying personal work values; and
- career placement and follow-up services.

(Adapted from Engels 1994)

In many ways, the key to effectiveness is not in offering each of the NCDA's five suggested services in isolation, but in offering all of them as part of a process. While Wessel (1998) discussed this need in college-level career centers, the thoughts easily translate to all centers: "We must be able to help students not only identify skills and interests, but to also inform students how those skills and interests are used in a work setting. We must maintain an active network of employer and alumni contacts in order to keep current." When the modern career center gives its clients the *tools* to succeed, when it teaches and assists in career development instead of job placement, it fulfills the mandate it has received from the modern world of work.

This book is designed, quite simply, to help today's career centers fulfill that mandate. Whether you are planning and developing a career center from scratch or overhauling an existing entity, blessed with resources or operating under appreciable constraints, serving a small and specific population or a large and varied one, this book can help. It follows a simple, four-stage process: planning, developing, implementing, and improving. Integrated within the process are such topics as marketing, access, and technology, so that they are not viewed in isolation.

The *planning* stage involves formulating both a philosophical foundation and concrete strategy for producing the functioning physical entity. Chapters One and Two take you through this stage by providing more information on the role of today's career centers and raising the questions and concerns that each center must address.

The second stage, *developing*, works out the practical aspects of creating (or recreating, as the case may be) a career center. Chapters Three through Five seek to turn your plans for the physical center into reality by addressing issues of space and furnishings, materials, and management of the facility.

A well-furnished, efficiently run center is no success unless it effectively connects to its target clientele—and that is the aim of the third stage, *implementing*. Chapters Six through Nine address the needs of career centers serving different populations in various environments.

The final stage of planning and developing a career center is *improving* it. Chapter Ten provides an action plan that concludes with an assessment of the center's room for improvement. Lest you think that the developmental work on your career center is at an end, you will find that there really is always room for improvement—and that the way to improve your center is to return to stage one.

Chapters Eleven and Twelve address concerns facing career centers in the very near future, specifically virtual, or online, centers and additional changes that are already beginning to affect the world of work. These items should be in the back of your mind as you work through each stage of constructing your career center.

Rather than feel intimidated or threatened by the changes and indeed the pace of change in the modern world of work, career center personnel can confidently undertake their important and challenging mission of helping individuals to create their own fulfilling and dynamic careers.

Summary

Over the past two decades, career centers have shifted their focus from matching people with jobs to facilitating lifelong career planning and learning. Effective career centers provide means of self-appraisal, career information, career counseling services, career training facilities, and career placement and follow-up services. To reach this level of comprehensiveness, career centers must set in motion a cyclical process of planning, developing, implementing, and improving.

Chapter 1

Career Development and the Role of Career Centers

by Don Schutt

It is the role of the modern career center to support and empower individuals to create and use personally meaningful career plans. Career centers can help individuals become "more self-directed and proactive in their own promotions and advancements, to make their needs known, [and] to empower themselves" (Hansen 1997). To better understand the career development process and the role of career centers, it is important first to define the conceptual components.

Conceptual Components

The following concepts provide the foundation on which effective career centers operate. Identifying the meanings of concepts early in the process and creating a shared set of definitions can decrease miscommunication and misdirection as the program grows. The terms career, career development, career guidance, and career counseling all have had variable meanings over the past two decades, the latter two terms generally changing to reflect the other two. As Hansen (1997) noted that "both anecdotal sources and formal surveys reveal that the public still views 'career' primarily as 'job' and that the outcome of vocational planning is often choosing a job," these clarifications are necessary to provide an effective delivery of services and also to educate career center users.

Career has been defined as a "life style concept that involves a sequence of work or leisure activities in which one engages throughout a lifetime. A career is unique to each person and is dynamic and unfolding throughout life. Careers include not only occupations but prevocational and postvocational activities and decisions as well as how persons integrate their work life with

5

their other life roles such as family, community and leisure pursuits. A career may include many occupations and jobs" (Ettinger 1996a). More simply, Ross (1995) described a career as the "sum of a person's experiences over the course of a lifetime," and reinforced the notion that career needs are interwoven with personal and social needs. "This concept recognizes that our jobs don't exist in isolation from the rest of our lives. In a single career, someone may have been a student, a plumber, an engineering technologist, a mother and a semi-retired consultant" (Ross 1995). This is in contrast to the definition of a *job,* which has been defined as "a group of similar paid positions requiring some similar attributes in a single organization" (Super 1976 as cited in Herr and Cramer 1996). These definitions portray a career as more personal than jobs held or the occupations in which an individual has been involved.

One of the challenges that career centers face is that of increasing user understanding of what now comprises the career development process. "The narrow definitions of career as job and of career planning as fitting into a job—the old linear model—are often still used. It is hard to change the mindset. In this scenario, people scan the environment for information and compete for their piece of a limited pie rather than see multiple possibilities in themselves and in society, in work and in all of life's roles" (Hansen 1997). As the definition of a career has expanded, so has the complexity of career development. These complexities challenge the perceptions and expectations of many providers and users within career development service delivery systems.

Career development has been defined as "the process by which one develops and refines self- and career-identity, work maturity and the ability to plan. It represents all the career-related choices and outcomes through which every person must pass. Indeed career development is generally conceived as a lifelong process through which individuals come to understand themselves as they relate to the world of work and their role in it" (Schilling, Schwallie-Giddis, and Giddis 1995). Gysbers (1996) expanded the definition to include the life roles outside of the workplace because career development

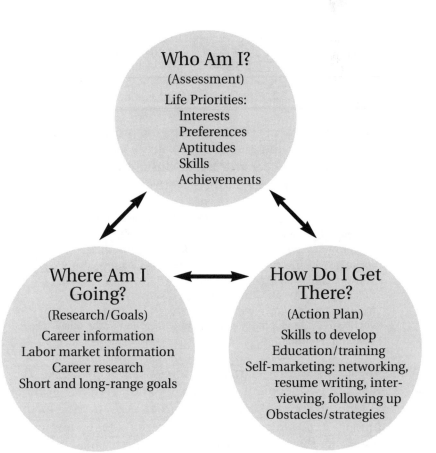

Figure 1.

The Three Critical Questions

...is a lens through which clients can view and understand work and family concerns. Add the factors of gender, ethnic origin, race, and religion and the lens becomes even more powerful. Now clients have a way of bringing their personal histories and the histories of their reference groups into focus. Now they can see how these factors have directly or indirectly influenced them, their views of themselves, others, and the world in which they live. Now they have four additional factors to use to understand and respond to their struggles with work and family issues and concerns.

Herr and Cramer (1996) reinforced both the progressive nature of career development and the crucial role of envisioning career development from the perspective of the individual rather than from the narrow job placement perspective:

[Career development includes] the lifelong behavioral processes and the influences on them that lead to one's work values, choice of occupation(s), creation of a career pattern, decision-making style, role integration, self-identity and career identity, educational literacy, and related phenomena. Career development proceeds—smoothly, jaggedly, positively, negatively—whether or not career guidance or career education exists. As such, career development is not an intervention but the object of an intervention.

While these definitions clarify the foundational concepts, they also guide the development of programs and services for career centers. One of the challenges that career centers face in their development is disputing perceptual barriers that view career development as the process of finding that first, single job. That perception leads to career centers that only provide information and guidance in finding the "perfect fit" between skills and jobs, ignoring life roles, continuous learning, and the responsibility of individuals in their career development processes. Borchard (1995) provided some insight into historical factors and the related attitudinal barriers that might influence an individual's approach to career development (and thereby influence their expectations of career centers). This information can be useful in helping individuals to recognize and consider how transitions in the world of work impact personal definitions of career and career development.

Borchard (1995) suggested that society is currently in a transition period between the end of one era (the Mass Production Era, which began in 1865 and ended in the 1980s) and the beginning of the next era (the Knowledge-Service Era, which started in the 1980s and extends to the present time). "The structural changes engulfing us over the past couple of decades have transformed our world from a corporation-centered and manufacturing-based order (the Mass Production Era) to that of a predominantly service-based, technology- and information-driven system (the Knowledge-Service Era)" (Borchard 1995). He suggested that the changing economy and changing work environment have placed different demands on future employees than were placed on previous generations. These changing demands have a widespread impact.

- The job-market structure has changed from a two-tiered factory system where blue collar workers were dominated by white collar workers (and some K-12 schools were organized to prepare students for one of two options—go to college or go to work) to a system of multi-tiered (or no tiered) structures where discussions of "gold collar workers" who possess a combination of technical competence and conceptual knowledge are increasing (for which the school-to-work movement is attempting to prepare students).
- The source for employment has shifted from one organization for the entire work life to multiple employers over an individual's career.
- The few stable, classifiable types of occupational characteristics are being replaced by many rapidly evolving occupational characteristics.
- It used to be that individuals completed their education (at whatever level) and went to work; increasingly, there has been a shift to continuous learning over the lifespan, particularly considering the rapid, continuous growth of technology.
- In the past, people got jobs through family ties (blue collar) or through classified ads and resumes (white collar). In the Knowledge-Service Era, however, developing indi-

vidual skills and competencies and ongoing networking are becoming more important.

- Career choices now are reached less through luck and happenstance and more through decision making and ongoing attention to the changing workplace.

(Condensed from Borchard 1995)

Two major elements arise from the comparison of career development in the Mass Production Era to career development in the Knowledge-Service Era that should be highlighted for both users and staff in career centers.

First, there is the contrast between the organization controlling (or guiding) the career development process for the individual and the individual managing her or his own career. In the Mass Production Era, once an individual was employed, her or his career path was "taken care of" by the employer. Lifelong employment might then have been guaranteed, but that changed in the 1980s when employees were put out of work, often by the same companies that had previously fostered the individual's development. This shift triggered two important revelations: "first, that the time had arrived when we could and needed to assume greater personal autonomy over our individual futures, and second, that we could design and develop careers that capitalized on our unique interests, talents, and personalities" (Borchard 1995). The implication is that as individuals assume the role of career manager, they need direction and assistance different from that provided in the past, when the emphasis was on finding a single job.

Second, this transition from the old era to the new one highlights the importance of individuals' ability to identify skills and transfer them from one environment to another. This becomes critical as individuals look to enter or progress in the workplace. Individuals demonstrate that capacity by reviewing experiences, identifying the skills developed through those experiences, and then applying those skills to new situations. Career centers can contribute by

- teaching the process of skill identification and transfer-ability of skills to multiple environments (and jobs),
- creating opportunities through collaborative agreements with employers or service organizations through which individuals can explore jobs/occupations and test their skills, and
- encouraging individuals to learn and then practice the skills they identify as important to the future.

While many recognize that the world of work, fuelled by the influx of technology and increased access to information, has changed dramatically, few recognize the influence of these changes on career development. Career centers can impact their communities by confronting the perceptual boundaries through education and the development of programs/services that represent a broader approach to career development.

A simpler way to characterize the career development process at the individual level is to view career development as the ongoing, overlapping process of seeking the answers to three questions: *Who am I?*, *Where am I going?*, and *How do I get there?* (Figure 1). This graphic captures the essence of the career development process. The *Who am I?* component encourages individuals to consider the personal characteristics brought to the process. The *Where am I going?* component involves the gathering, consolidation, and synthesis of information from the world of work with personal characteristics. Those two components combine together and are projected into the future through the *How do I get there?* planning component.

In the Mass Production Era, career development consisted primarily of *Where am I going?* and *How do I get there?*, and the process ended once one arrived at the work experience. In the Knowledge-Service Era, the circle represents recycling through the process of answering the three questions. This continuous loop of self-knowledge (Who am I?), educational and occupational exploration (Where am I going?), and career planning (How do I get there?) is also supported and specified more thoroughly in the National Career Development competencies and indicators.

The National Career Development Guidelines (NCDG) were developed by the National Occupational Information Coordinating Committee (NOICC) in 1996 to stimulate state and local communities to create comprehensive career development programs. The three main components of the guidelines are: K-adult career development competencies, counselor competencies, and program capabilities. These guidelines were endorsed by the American Counseling Association, the American School Counselor Association, the American Vocational Association Guidance Division, the National Association of State Career Development/Guidance Supervisors, and the National Career Development Association. Career centers have the responsibility of providing developmentally appropriate activities and processes to users and centers can use the K-adult competency structure to identify career-related developmental tasks for individuals at four levels: elementary, middle school/junior high school, high school, and adult.

The competency structure is further broken into three major career development areas related to the career development process: self-knowledge, educational and occupational exploration, and career planning. For each area, competencies are delineated to address the developmental needs of individuals at each level. In total, there are twelve competencies identified in the NCDG. Because this model is developmentally based, the assumption is that as individuals progress through various developmental stages they become more sophisticated in using the skills identified in the competencies and through the indicators.

The organization of each competency (each of the twelve competencies numbered as they are in the guidelines) within the three major areas is:

> Self-Knowledge Area:
> 1. Demonstrate a positive self-concept
> 2. Work with others
> 3. Accept growth and change
> Educational and Occupational Exploration Area:
> 4. Education and skills
> 5. Work and learning

6. Information and planning
7. Personal responsibility and work habits
8. Work and society
Career Planning Area:
9. Make decisions
10.Balance life roles
11.Understand the influences in society
12.Develop career plans

In addition, there are two or more indicators for each competency at each level. The indicators can be used to identify whether an individual has developed the skills in the competency area. The competencies are listed in bold print and identified by a single number; indicators related to each competency at each level are identified by points below each competency. For example, at the Elementary Level in the area of Self-Knowledge the first competency is

1. Knowledge of the importance of self-concept.

There are six indicators that take the form of skills or activities that students demonstrate to verify their knowledge of the importance of self-concept. The first indicator is:

1.1 Describe positive characteristics about self as seen by self and others.

Elementary-age students who are able to describe their positive characteristics might be considered partially competent in the area of self-concept. All of the competencies can be used to identify career development needs (or goals), which can then serve as a guide for developing programs and services relevant to individual career development needs.

While it is important for career centers to connect to national initiatives like the NCDG, there may also be state, local, or population-specific models that can be used to provide direction and support to the development and implementation of the career center. Many states have developmental guidance models through which school counseling programs work with teachers to provide activities that help students progress in specific developmental areas. For example, the state of Wisconsin has a developmental guidance model consisting of nine competency areas that suggest that students can: connect family, school, and work; solve problems; understand diversity, inclusiveness, and fairness; work in groups; manage conflict; integrate growth and development; direct change; make decisions; and set and achieve goals (Schutt, Brittingham, Perrone, Bilzing, and Thompson 1997).

A clear conceptualization of career and career development is important when developing programs and services in career centers. Centers can work with individuals to organize these concepts (particularly the answers to *Who am I?*, *Where am I going?*, and *How do I get there?*) through the creation and maintenance of an individual career plan. Career plans that are developed individually and represent the career development process can be useful in encouraging center users to become managers of their own career development.

Career plans are developed in many ways and come in a variety of forms. Portfolio-planners illustrate one form that is often used by schools but just as frequently overlooked by adults. NOICC has developed an adult portfolio-planning system for adults hoping to increase their knowledge and skills in the area of career planning. Portfolios are useful in providing structure to the career development process and can direct individuals through the following steps:

- Guide individuals through identifying their skills, interests, and abilities.
- Encourage them to process that information to identify occupational areas that might be of interest.
- Have them investigate the occupations, paying particular attention to skill areas that they might need to enhance if they wish to pursue a particular occupational area.
- Once a choice has been identified, encourage them to use the planning component to search for a workplace experience to "test" out a job in the occupational area.
- Depending on the outcome of the experience, plot a course for entry detailed through the portfolio-planner.

- Continuously return to the portfolio-planner to update success and project new areas necessary to continue growing, developing, and preparing for the changing world of work.

Again, portfolio-planners are but one of the many tools that can be created to respond to the changing demands in this Knowledge-Service Era. Regardless of form, the plans should help individuals to synthesize the information needed to make effective decisions about the development of their career. Viewing career development as a lifelong process directs the type of information that needs to be gathered and the consideration it needs to be given.

In general, career centers can assist individuals in making career decisions and developing plans that consolidate past experiences, identify existing personal (likes, dislikes, interests, skills, abilities, past work successes, and aptitudes) and situational (family demands, economic needs, geographic preferences, future dreams) variables, and use this information to chart a course for the future that examines skills and interests applicable across possibly many different jobs or occupations. While the outcome might be individuals' naming a single job or occupational area, the goal should be to help them identify a number of opportunities and to integrate lifelong learning into the plan.

Implications for Career Centers

From the previous discussion, five implications emerge as career centers look to engage in providing services.

1. There is a critical need to educate staff, advisory boards, and users on the changing needs of individuals relative to career development. Although it has become evident that career development must be a self-directed, lifelong process, this still has not been incorporated into the training of many career professionals and the operations of many career centers. They are still operating according to the old linear model of assessing skills and matching them with job openings.

It is important to challenge that model because to work oblivious to the modern definition of career development as a lifelong process may adversely affect the services offered and ultimately the lives of center users. McDaniels and Gysbers (1992) addressed this more specifically when they noted the problem of individual assessments made in the traditional model seeking to predict which educational or employment opportunities would be most suitable. While prediction must remain a part of the modern career development process, it must be supplemented by methods of exploring and expanding all of the individual's interests and abilities.

2. Keep the goals and objectives of the center consistent with the goals and objectives of career development. Remember that "careers are unique to each person and created by what one chooses or does not choose. They are dynamic and unfold throughout life. They include not only occupations but prevocational and postvocational concerns as well as integration of work with other roles: family, community, leisure" (Herr and Cramer 1996). Provide services beyond the traditional individual assessments, career and labor market information, and placement. Teach career development processes and reiterate the individual's need for continuously answering the three questions of *Who am I?*, *Where am I going?*, and *How do I get there?* Regardless of the setting of your career center, the goals and objectives must also be kept in line with those of the institution to which you are connected, either physically or financially.

3. Be clear as to what the center can and cannot offer. Do not mislead users by suggesting that the services provided are comprehensive if they are not. If the center can offer assessment services and career information, for example, it should make clear to its users that they are not receiving placement assistance and then refer them to centers that do help with placement. Likewise, if the center cannot offer Internet access or CD-ROM capabilities, it should make users aware of these resources and suggest where they might go to take advantage of them. Simple decency demands that centers be honest with their users, but this kind of honesty about the range of services offered also leads users to form realistic expectations and expand their knowledge of what is available to them.

16

4. *Teach individuals to become managers of their own career development process.* As the pattern of determining one's career has changed, so must the ownership of the career development process. In the past, it was permissable for individuals to find one job and let their employer direct their careers from then on. That simply does not happen today. Employees no longer feel tied to their employers and employers no longer direct the careers of their employees; as Hansen (1997) noted, "the most frequent estimate is that the average adult will make five to seven major career changes in a lifetime." Clearly, individuals need to take charge of their own career development and take action to ensure that their needs and desires are met, their abilities and interests put to good use. Career centers can support this by providing the tools that individuals need to make fully informed, workable decisions at every stage of their lives.

5. *Create tools such as an individualized personal career plan.* Employing career plans as a method for individuals to steer their paths is consistent with the career development process being managed at the individual level. Formalize the process as well as the tools for use with the center's intended audience, recognizing their needs and the developmental level (using the NCDG and other modern guidelines as a gauge) at which they enter the system. Regardless of your target audience or your experience in career center development, it is important to consult with other career centers to gain a deeper understanding of how these processes and tools can work. If your center does not have the resources necessary to offer the construction of individual career plans (or similar tools), it is best to work with other centers or contract with other professionals to provide them.

Career Centers and Career Development

The specific role of career centers relative to career development is left ultimately to the developer of the center. While the specifics are yet to be determined, there are common themes that should run through centers.

Career centers should serve as facilitators of the career development process. Most importantly, the services offered and the method of utilization should teach individuals the process of learning about themselves and the world of work, challenging old paradigms of their role in that world. It is important to teach new processes (answering the three questions) not utilized or necessarily understood by many adults who entered the world of work during the Mass Production Era. Their experiences—and the experiences of their role models—may not reflect existing realities. For example, an adult may have utilized family connections to secure a position at the same company where their relatives worked. If the company closes, that person is not only unemployed but also limited by his or her solitary, outmoded concept of how to pursue a career. Such an adult could greatly benefit from a career center intervening to teach the career development process (including the concept of lifelong learning) as a part of the effort to assist in finding new work. By teaching the process, the career center meets the immediate needs to find work while also preparing the individual for future job transitions over the course of their careers.

Another related theme is the synthesis of information used to make career decisions and to develop career plans. At one time, access to information was a critical issue. With the advent of the Internet and other methods of quickly transmitting large quantities of information, however, the problem is no longer one of access but of managing the information to make sense of it on a personal level. Career centers can teach individuals how to use new technologies to gather information and, more importantly, consolidate and personalize the information to meet the individuals' career development needs. Only after determining what those needs are and how the individuals' interests and abilities come into play can centers really help clients determine what career and labor market information is relevant and useful.

Finally, career centers can serve as resource centers for their communities. Partnership and collaborative projects should be developed to connect the center with others contributing to the career development of individuals in the community. This can help to identify new contributors, to garner support for the center, and ultimately to connect center users with the world of work.

It is both interesting and important to note that each of the varied and meaningful roles the career center plays is always a supporting role. Career centers can and do make a real difference in the lives of those who seek help and guidance at various stages of their careers. Still, it must be stated that the individual clients bear ultimate responsibility for their career choices and the results—good and bad—their decisions bring.

Summary

CONCEPTUAL COMPONENTS
- A career is the sequence of occupational and leisure activities unique to each person.
- A job is just a paid position or a group of similar paid positions.
- Career development is the lifelong process of career and personal decision-making.
- The Mass Production Era (1865 to the 1980s) was marked by single, stable careers guided by employers.
- The Knowledge-Service Era (the 1980s to the present) is marked by multiple, diverse careers guided by employees.

The career development process of the individual can be characterized as the ongoing process of asking the following questions:

- Who am I?
- Where am I going?
- How do I get there?

IMPLICATIONS FOR CAREER CENTERS
- Recognize the critical need to educate staff, advisory boards, and users on the changing career development needs of individuals.
- Keep the goals and objectives of the center consistent with the goals and objectives of career development.
- Be clear as to what the center can and cannot offer.
- Teach individuals to become managers of their own career development processes.
- Create tools such as an individualized personal career plan.

Chapter 2

Assessment and Evaluation: Understanding Who You Serve

by Don Schutt and Steve Bialek

Determining who your center serves is a vital question to answer in the beginning stages of development. It impacts logistical questions such as location and hours of service as well as the method of delivering services. Exploring the needs of your audience and assessing the environment in which the center exists allows you to create goals that reflect the purpose of the center. Assessment and evaluation is an important process to continuously weave into all center activities; however, by regularly revisiting the question of service to the target audience, you can adapt the center to keep pace with a changing world and the changing needs of your clients.

This chapter looks at both program assessment and evaluation as a continuous planning and improvement process for career centers. Commonly, this process is seen as having a distinct beginning and ending (which is different than will be discussed here). As such, needs assessments are discussed at the beginning of development and evaluation is seen as the finale to the implementation process. However, when discussed as a planning and improvement process, both assessment and evaluation are closely connected, so that data can be collected continuously and used as a method for ongoing program planning and improvement.

The planning and improvement process begins with (1) needs assessment, which leads to (2) program planning, followed by (3) formative or process evaluation, and ending with (4) summative or outcome evaluation (Isaac and Michael 1984). These four steps continuously loop back to reviewing the needs of users and how the center can improve on delivering services to meet those needs (see Figure 2).

21

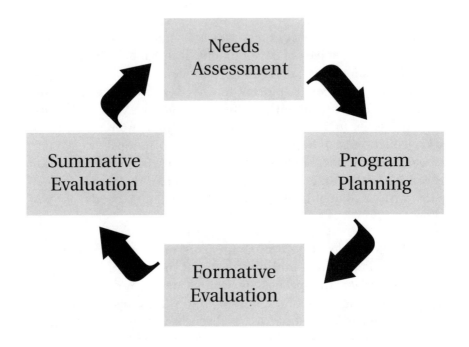

Figure 2.

The Planning and Improvement Process

It is important to begin the development of the center with the end in mind. In other words, decide early on what the center needs to understand about its users and services, and then build a process that will provide the answers to those questions while maintaining the flexibility to respond in a timely fashion to feedback and patterns not anticipated.

The Needs Assessment

The purpose of a needs assessment is to identify the issues from which the career center's mission, operating principles, vision, and goals emerge. Isaac and Michael support this purpose: "A need has been defined as the discrepancy between what is and what ought to be. Once identified, needs are placed in order of priority. They are the basis for setting program goals" (1984). Often, identified needs represent problems or challenges to be overcome, problems which could come in many forms.

Take as a simple but all too common example a college student who decides to be an elementary school teacher. As an undergraduate, she majors in education. During the student's senior year practice teaching, a problem arises when she realizes that working with young children is not to her liking. This problem might have been averted if the campus career center and the advising office had worked together to suggest that students explore potential majors through experiences in the workplace prior to making firm decisions. An even better solution would have been for the career center to establish relationships with employers or alumni in order to provide sites at which students could meet those exploratory needs. This problem or need, transformed to a program goal, might lead the center to develop closer working relationships with existing campus departments that provide students with advising related to occupational or career goals.

The National Career Development Guidelines (NCDG) provide a framework for better understanding the *what ought to be*. While the guidelines focus on creating comprehensive career development programs through competencies and indicators (discussed in Chapter 1), the guidelines also detail three career development program areas: content, processes, and structure. *Content* is defined by NOICC (1985b) as the standards—state, local, or both—organized around the three broad areas of self-knowledge, educational and occupational exploration, and career planning. *Processes* are the strategies that actually deliver the program content, and *structure* is the framework supporting the programs' activities. The structure includes organizing the planning of the program, clarifying staff roles and responsibilities, securing resources, monitoring program delivery, and revising the program.

NCDG Program Components

Program Content Areas:
    Self-Knowledge
    Educational and Occupational Exploration
    Career planning
Program Delivery Processes:
    Outreach
    Instruction
    Counseling
    Assessment
    Career information
    Work experience
    Placement
    Consultation
    Referral
    Follow-up
Program Structure:
    Leadership
    Program Management
    Personnel
    Facilities
    Resources
(NOICC 1995b)

These program areas provide career centers with a framework to understand *what ought to be* in place as well as a strategy for organizing components within a program. These areas also translate to the operation of a career center as they address the questions of

(1) What are we delivering (content)? (2) How is that content going to be delivered (processes)? and (3) How will we achieve this within our organizational structure (structure)?

The program content areas and the program delivery processes draw directly from the needs assessment discussed in this section. Initially, the center's leadership and program management structure may already be in place as the needs assessment process begins (in fact, they may be responsible for the process). The needs assessment serves to clarify issues related to the delivery process, staffing requirements, facilities, and resources required to complete the center. A thorough assessment of the needs of the community (or environment) and of the individual user provides the foundation for the center.

Identifying Community and Environment Issues

What is known about the environment where the career center will be located? Are other services currently offered in the community? Are those services offered to some people but not to others? Is there support for the career center or is it seen as competing with existing services or programs? Who will collaborate with the center to create a seamless system of delivery? In schools, is there a developmental guidance program that has a career component in place? Who has access and who needs access to the services a career center can provide? While some career centers are established to meet specific demands within a community (like students making the transitions from education to employment or civilians readjusting after military base closures), other centers operate to serve the needs of entire cities and counties. Regardless of the context, it is important to have a sense of the role the center plays in the community.

The community and environment components to be assessed include: attitudes about career centers; political climate in the community regarding career development; number of community-based organizations, technical colleges, or other organizations providing services; resources available internally and externally, and the ability to collaborate with school programs (even for centers serving populations other than K-12 students). It also includes questions of access to and support from local business partners, postsecondary educational institutions, other training programs, and various community agencies.

Gysbers and Henderson (1994) provided one example of a community and environment assessment that demonstrated an exhaustive process for schools to follow when developing a comprehensive developmental school guidance program. While their example was directed at developing a school guidance program, there is significant overlap between that endeavor and the task of developing a comprehensive career center. The advice of Gysbers and Henderson is worth noting:

> The efficiency of a program is measured in terms of the ratio of resources applied to the benefits accrued. Thus, gathering concrete information about the resources available and used in the guidance program is essential to any program decisions to be made. The more complete your knowledge of the resources currently available, the more room you have for creativity as you decide to redirect them for program improvements and the more specific you can be in your requests for additional resources.

They went on to define resources in three different areas: human, financial, and political. In the area of human resources, they studied student-to-counselor ratios and provided a succinct description of a counselor time study used to evaluate the allotment of time appropriated to each of four counseling program task areas. Those areas had been identified earlier in the process as comprising the counseling program content area. The financial resources were identified as budget expenditures, existing materials and equipment, and facilities, so they were prepared in case additional space was needed for workshops or other activities. The political resources evaluated were policy statements made at the school, district, community, state, and federal levels. From this assessment, gaps were identified and a determination was made regarding the support that could be expected as the program advanced through the development and planning stages.

Assessing the community climate for potential collaboration with and support for the center needs to be given high consideration as goals are developed. Of equal importance is gaining insights into the services that potential users currently need as well as predicting the services that users might request once the center is available.

Understanding Individual Needs

The career needs of individuals are diverse. Clarifying the gaps in existing services and exploring the possibilities for services never before considered are included in the assessment of individual needs. While the previous assessment of the community and environment entailed a consideration of attitudes, resources, and connections, the assessment of individual needs focuses on who the center's users are and what they want. Brown and Brown (1990) recommended that individual needs assessment be designed to collect information in the following domains:

1. whether there is a desire for assistance with career planning;
2. preferred type of assistance with career planning (e.g., individual counseling);
3. types of career information needed; and
4. special need[s].

The first domain, "desire for assistance with career planning," focused on how many people expect to access the career center. It also set out to provide an estimate of when individuals might participate if various types of career development activities were offered. Interest in participating in career development programming should be elicited during the needs assessment. Questions that might help generate this type of information are: Are you interested in exploring career opportunities at this time? Are you planning to use a career center to explore career opportunities within the next three months? Six months? Determining the desire for career assistance achieves two goals. One, of course, is whether individuals would consider coming to a career center to explore career opportunities. The second, perhaps not as obvious a goal, is to provoke the thought in individuals that a career center is a resource for meeting their career development needs.

The second area, "preferred types of assistance," gauged individuals' preferred delivery process. Brown and Brown (1990) suggested that potential users should be queried with regard to the manner they would prefer to access career development services. Examples included individual career counseling, group career exploration activities, and self-directed activities such as using a computer. This is directly connected to the processes that the center envisions in terms of service delivery. Through this assessment, it might be discovered that there is no interest in working in groups but great interest in individual counseling, and this will shape the type of services the center will provide.

"Types of career information needed" was the third area. This required a better understanding of the specific reasons for a user to come to the center. Are they seeking information about a particular occupation? Perhaps they want to know what the demand will be for a given occupation five years from now. Employing the three content areas from the National Career Development Guidelines, it might be possible to stimulate user interest in investigating the other two areas of self-knowledge or career planning (in addition to the area related to educational and occupational information that brought them to the center). This also provides an opportunity to educate individuals with the Mass Production Era view of career development about the changing nature of workplaces and approaches to career development.

Lastly, "identifying special needs" refers to necessary adaptations in the center with such items as adapted computer screens, captioned video and computer segments, desk heights that facilitate wheel chair access, assistance in retrieving materials from shelves, or restrooms with accessible stalls. This area addresses questions of access and user-oriented services. Special needs might also include bilingual staff, or staff familiar with issues related to second-generation students. These special needs might also direct the types of resources and services that a center offers based on the types of information sought by different groups.

Identifying and understanding how to respond to many different needs posed by the variety of individual developmental career needs is challenging. A basic student needs survey should collect individual information in five different areas: academic needs, career, special topics, preferred activities, and comments.

Carefully determine the individual information needed to help build a profile of potential users of the career center and consider how that information fits with the results of the community and environmental assessment. Career center staff should determine what the priority is—individual needs, community needs, or both—and then shape the center based on those priorities.

Collecting Information (Data Collection)

There are many different ways to collect data. The methods used to gather data typically either expand the breadth of knowledge regarding a topic or seek to deepen understanding. Planning the data collection process is critical as it ensures that the information collected is both useful and thorough. The NCDG recommend a format for planning the needs assessment:

1. Identify the participants.
   Which groups will be assessed?
   How will these groups be sampled?
   Based on expected return, how many people do we need to have in the sample?
2. Finalize the needs assessment method.
   Does the recommended needs assessment instrument meet our needs? If not, how should it be modified?
   What alternative forms do we want to develop for specific groups?
   Will respondents be willing to respond to the entire instrument or should we divide the competencies into two instruments?
   How should we format the instrument so it is easy to score?
3. Collect data.
   How will the instruments be administered? Will we use a different approach for different groups?
   Who will be responsible for administering the instrument to each group?
   What is our time schedule for administration?
   How many follow-ups will we do? When should they be done? How will we do them?
4. Analyze data.

How will we determine what competencies and indicators were rated most and least important?

How will we determine whether the results differed by group?

How can we report the results to various groups?

(Condensed from Kobylarz 1996)

The NCDG example provides general tips for developing a plan to assess and evaluate the competencies and indicators as a measure of individual needs. The assumption, while not explicit, is that a paper-and-pencil instrument will be administered. Brown and Brown (1990) suggested the following process for conducting an assessment based on a needs assessment questionnaire:

1. Use a committee that is generally familiar with the potential users of the [career center] to draft the questionnaire. Include some of the potential users (e.g., students, employees) on the committee.
2. Field test the questionnaire to make sure that questions are understood and provide the data needed.
3. When possible, use answer sheets that can be scanned and tabulated by a computer to save time.
4. Keep the questionnaire as short as possible. The longer the questionnaire, the lower the return rate.
5. Disseminate the information to potential users of the [career center:] counselors, managers/administrators, and others who have a need to know.
6. Rank the needs as one means of establishing priorities for the center. Typically, needs are ranked on the basis of the number of people expressing a need (e.g., 100 people want more information about high-tech occupations), but the needs of minorities, women, and the physically handicapped should receive high priority.

(Brown and Brown 1990)

The distinction between these two examples is a focus on the content of the instrument under development in one (NCDG) and a focus on a process for developing the assessment in the other (Brown and Brown). Both of these examples describe data collection procedures that collect a breadth of information that can be analyzed to find patterns from which individual needs can be identified.

When the plan calls for a greater depth of information, interviews, focus groups and informal conversations are useful data collection methods. The advantages of each must be considered along with limitations, but thorough planning and preparation increases the effectiveness of any data collection method.

Interviews can be formally structured, or they can be open-ended and nondirect. The advantage of interviews is that they are flexible and can result in a greater understanding of participant responses. For example, a survey of a broad community audience may reveal that 95 percent of potential center users feel isolated during a job search. However, interviews focusing on depth would allow respondents to explain what "isolated" means to them. For one person it might mean an extended delay sitting in an employer's reception area. For another, it might mean long evenings alone writing cover letters. Disadvantages of interviews include the fact that they take longer to conduct, data analysis can be challenging, and variation in interviewer skills may produce inconsistent results.

Focus group sessions are an efficient means to gather individual information, particularly as related to investment of time. Focus groups also allow for a natural synergy to occur among participants resulting in more meaningful information than if individual interviews were conducted with each person. Two drawbacks of this type of method include the high skill level needed by session facilitators and the difficulty of performing data analysis.

A third, often overlooked method is conversation with colleagues, friends, family and acquaintances. This informal approach calls for identifying and communicating with those people in the community who are well connected and who can provide insight into a variety of needs. This notion of utilizing insights from the community is not a new one; Knowles (1978) suggested that opinions of experts and people in helping roles be sought to identify needs they perceive as widespread among potential participants.

The purpose in gathering information is to begin to identify areas where career centers can have an impact either by enhancing existing services or by revealing new opportunities. In consolidating the data into a report, consider analyzing the need or problem. The following questions assist in formulating a response or goal:

1. What is the problem or need identified? (Summarize it in a sentence.)
2. What is happening? (Describe the present situation.)
3. What should be happening? (Describe applicable standards, objectives, policies.)
4. What is the gap between what is happening and what should be happening? (Explain it as precisely as possible.)
5. How important is the difference between what is happening and what should be happening? (Describe costs of the problem or consequences if left unattended, as well as you can anticipate them.)
6. What causes the difference between what is happening and what should be happening? (Describe briefly whether it is caused by a deficiency in knowledge, skills, or the environment.)
7. What is the appropriate solution to the problem? (Explain how the career center can meet the need identified.)
8. What will be the likely impact of the solution on the community or organization? (Describe possible positive and negative consequences of any proposed solution and then explain how to head off the negative consequences.)

(Adapted from Rothwell and Kazanas 1992)

By systematically applying these questions, a goal statement can be developed that addresses the opportunities and needs to which the career center will respond. Ultimately, the mission of the center along with programmatic goals should be developed and prioritized through the needs assessment process.

Program Planning

The words *mission, purpose, charter,* and *role* are often used interchangeably to describe this first step in the planning process. A clear definition of mission is a prerequisite to planning for a career center. While there is no standard way to write a mission statement, these elements are often included:

- Why—The main reason for the career center to exist
- What—The products or services
- Who—The customer, client, consumer or market served
- Where—The primary scope and/or boundaries of the organization

Goals are "broadly philosophical, global, relatively timeless, and nonmeasurable" (Isaac and Michael 1984) statements about center activities, services, or processes. The program planning phase expands on the goals created from the needs assessment.

Program planning responds with action to the goals developed through the needs assessment. "From program goals, specific measurable objectives are derived and a plan containing the means to attain these objectives—the program procedures, strategies, and activities—is formulated" (Isaac and Michael 1984). Simply put, "the evaluation of the [center] actually begins when the objectives (1) address a need, (2) tell what program is to be employed to meet that need, (3) identify a date by which the program is to be completed, and (4) establish a criterion for success" (Brown and Brown 1990).

One level of specificity among goals and objectives was demonstrated in this excerpt from a report on the development of a high school career center.

Expected Outcomes
1. Fifty of the one hundred high school teachers will sign out materials from the career education resource center.
2. Fifty of the one hundred teachers will write a summary of how the career education center materials assisted their classroom lessons.
3. Seventy of one hundred randomly selected seniors will indicate a college major or career direction on their final plans.

Measurement of Outcome
1. Over a twelve week period a circulation record will show that fifty of the one hundred high school teachers have

used the career education center to obtain materials for their classroom lessons.

2. Over a twelve week period fifty of the one hundred high school teachers will write a summary of how they used the career education materials to improve their classroom lessons.

3. At the end of the twelve-week period, when presented with a survey, seventy of one hundred randomly selected seniors will be able to indicate either a college major or career direction on their final plans.

(Adapted from Zalinsky 1993)

In this particular program, these outcome statements directed the development of the program down to the forms for keeping records, including the follow-up surveys to teachers.

Once the objectives have been defined, intervention strategies, activities, and delivery processes should be identified. Choosing the most appropriate strategy for achieving the goals and meeting the objectives requires consideration for the instructional mode used to facilitate the career development process. Many choices exist in terms of delivery, from face-to-face individual contacts to groups and from distance education to computer-based training. The following questions can guide centers toward selecting an effective mode (or modes) of instruction.

1. How do the performance objectives connect to the content?

2. What basic instructional strategies (or processes) do you think would be most suitable for achieving these objectives with the people you will be working with, taking account of all relevant factors?

3. Which processes should be adopted: outreach, instruction, counseling, assessment, career information, work experience, placement, consultation, or referral?

4. Of these processes, which does the center have the capacity to provide given the materials, facilities, and staff?

Centers may be prevented from providing some of these services by staff composition. In cases where the most effective instructional mode is not available at the center, it is the ethical responsibility of the center to refer the user to a qualified service provider.

The needs assessment should lead to the development of the program goals and objectives which are linked to the activities proposed by the center. These activities, connected to the three broad career development content areas of self-knowledge, educational and occupational exploration, and career planning, will also have been combined in the program planning stage with delivery processes that are within the perimeter of the center's capacity. It is at this stage that the career center is shifting into the implementation mode, and there is an ongoing assessment and evaluation of the overall program.

Formative Evaluation

Formative (sometimes referred to as *proactive* or *process*) evaluation is concerned with formulating an evaluation of instruction/delivery to facilitate ongoing program improvement and planning. In the formative evaluation process, both the progress toward the earlier identified objectives and the implementation should be evaluated. According to Isaac and Michael (1984), the evaluation of the implementation "seeks out discrepancies between the plan and the reality [and] keeps the program true to its design or modifies it appropriately." The evaluation of the process is distinguished from the evaluation of the outcomes as it "monitors indicators of progress [developed in the program planning stage] toward the objectives; makes mid-course corrections, as appropriate." The method of evaluation may take many forms, similar to those discussed in the data collection section.

Again, formative evaluation is intended to measure progress toward goals and to search for problems in the implementation of the center. The key to understanding formative evaluation is recognizing that it is the study of the center while in progress.

Summative Evaluation

Summative (also called *retroactive* or *product*) evaluation determines whether the goals have been met. It produces an overview of strengths and weaknesses that is the springboard for beginning the improvement process. It is conducted after results have been measured (therefore after the formative evaluation).

The summative evaluation should not only be concerned with whether the goals were achieved but also whether the goals were worth achieving. The Tennessee State Department of Education (1990) added: "Not only does it provide information on what needs to be added or deleted, what gets the most use and where to make improvements, but it also helps others in the support network to stay informed. Evaluation reports should be sent to all individuals involved in the Career Center." Similar to the various methods of data collection described in this chapter, summative evaluation might take the form of assessments, follow-up studies, interviews, observations, career portfolios, or some blend of these.

The purpose of summative evaluation is to certify program utility (Worthen and Sanders 1987). It is intended to appeal to potential consumers and/or funding agencies. Summative evaluation is often conducted by an external evaluator, attempts to "convince" the audience, is done with limited frequency, and is usually large in scale.

Summary

Understanding your career center's audience is critical to successful continuous planning and improvement. The four key steps in evaluating and meeting the needs of center users are

1. **Needs assessment.** This includes identifying community and environment issues and understanding the needs of individual users.
2. **Program planning.** This should begin with a general mission statement and evolve into outlining expected outcomes and the measurement of outcomes.

3. **Formative evaluation.** This is also called *process evaluation* because it assesses the ongoing processes of development and implementation.
4. **Summative evaluation.** This is also called *outcome evaluation* because it assesses the outcome of the planning and development activities.

To reinforce this notion of planning and evaluation as a continuous process, the chapters focusing on specific target audiences also discuss specific planning, assessment, and evaluation strategies. The intention is to encourage revisiting these issues periodically and within the context of the career center program.

Chapter 3

Developing Your Facilities

by Don Schutt

There are a number of questions that need to be answered as facilities are developed. The first is whether there is space already existing that has been identified as career center space. If the answer is yes, that space may guide the development process. If the answer is no, there may be more opportunities for creativity and design. This chapter focuses on the physical design of a career center, including consideration of equipment and technology needs.

Location

The physical location of the center is likely to impact use. The following suggestions should help to ensure that the location of your center produces a positive impact.

1. Be near the main flow of traffic. This means different things to different centers. One example from Waukesha, Wisconsin (near Milwaukee) came when the staff was developing a Workforce Development Center. They did not have a site selected or building space identified, so their criteria for the location selection process included

- Near Interstate 94 [a major highway in the area] transportation corridor on existing or logical extension of public transportation.
- Proximity to Waukesha and Milwaukee (population center) labor force.
- "Neutral" site outside major city locations.
- Site providing visibility and positive image.
                              (Workforce Development Center 1997)

Further, their evaluative criteria in the site selection process included items like "size of parcel," "land/topography," "soil conditions," "existing vegetation," and "architectural controls." While their specific needs might be different from those of other centers, the critical point is a location near the main flow of traffic. The Workforce Development Center found a site that met all their criteria on the Waukesha County Technical College grounds. The goal was to develop a community career center that combined community services with a career center. They achieved their goal. The building currently integrates the services of nine agencies and 110 employees and provides career services in about one-third of the building and career-related services in the remaining two-thirds.

In schools, the "main flow of traffic" area might translate to the main floor or near the cafeteria. Carefully choosing a physical location in your community, organization, or school provides both visibility for the center and easy entry for the users. If the goal is to have the center put to use, it is vital that it not be too far off the beaten path.

2. Be near the building entrance and close to parking. This also may differ depending on whether users will already be located in the building or whether they will need to find parking to visit. Recognize that new users may know how to get to your building but may not know how to get to the career center once inside. If the center is located away from the main entrance, be sure to prepare and post proper signage to direct potential users to the center. A negative experience getting to the center might prematurely end a visit.

3. Stay away from high noise levels. This pertains particularly to school or other settings where there is potential for noise from athletic or music events or classes that might intrude on work being done in the career center. This also relates to noise from heating/cooling systems, street traffic, or other interference from the outside environment. If the center is planning on providing individual assessment services, there should at least be a quiet room protected from distracting noise that might reduce the effectiveness of the assessment process.

4. Be near the offices of trained professional counselors or career development facilitators. Since career-related issues often overlap with life issues, it is important to consider how the center will respond when individuals need services or present questions and concerns that the center cannot address. Having counselors available as part of your center staff or in nearby offices is one strategy for alleviating this challenge. Madison East High School in Madison, Wisconsin, located the school counseling offices immediately adjacent to the career center. This offers students an opportunity to have contact with their counselors as they explore, investigate and plan for their careers. It also creates opportunities for counselors who are working with students to go to the career center and assist them in the career development process.

Choosing a location is an important task. Keep in mind the population that the center intends to service and choose a location that best fits those users' needs. Once a site is chosen, design and layout become the next critical considerations.

Design and Layout

The design and layout of a center is influenced by responses to the following questions.

1. What types of services does the center plan to offer? The services provided can assist in the design of the layout for a career center. The New Mexico State University Career Center divided the space into seven areas: the Career Resource Room, the Office of Career Planning Coordinator, the computer room, the Office of Placement Coordinator, the Job Opportunity Board, the college catalog collection, and the career center reception area.

2. How accessible is the center for individuals with disabilities? Designing an accessible site is important. Tindall, Gugerty, Thuli, Phelps, and Stoddard (1994) examined the needs of three groups of individuals—those with mobility impairments, those with visual impairments, and those with hearing impairments—relative to planning accessible conferences and meetings. They suggested the following points be considered (here adapted for career center use):

Individuals with Mobility Impairments

- Accessibility of main entrances to the site
- Doorways wide enough to accommodate wheelchairs and three-wheel carts of varying sizes
- Appropriately graded ramping in inaccessible areas (including meeting rooms and lounge areas)
- Wide spaces, corridors, and aisles
- Level surfaces
- Accessible restrooms (including wide doors, unobstructed sinks of appropriate height, large stalls, grab bars, adequate space in which to maneuver a wheelchair, and controls and equipment easily operated from a sitting position).
- Public telephones at accessible height
- Adequate space for wheelchairs in meeting rooms and at tables
- Wheelchair-accessible registration tables
- Electrical outlets, light switches, and closet rods of appropriate height

Individuals with Visual Impairments

- Well-lit areas with adjustable lighting
- Obstacle-free environment (i.e., free of protruding objects that cannot be detected easily)
- Large, tactile directions for equipment, elevators, and restrooms; elevator numbers written in braille or raised print

Individuals with Hearing Impairments

- Rooms equipped with alternative emergency devices such as visual alarms and indicators (i.e., flashing lights on doors, telephones, and fire alarms), volume-controlled phone lines, and close-captioned television
- An available TDD (telecommunication device for the deaf)

More specific details—from curb ramps to parking zone sizes to sinks—should not be overlooked. There are also a number of Internet sites that provide much greater detail regarding access (and the laws) for individual with disabilities. Check these three sites for more specific details:

- The U.S. Department of Justice (http://www.usdoj.gov/crt/ada/adahom1.htm)
- The U.S. Access Board, also known as the Architectural and Transportation Barriers Compliance Board (http://www.access-board.gov/bfdg/adaag.htm)
- Association of Science-Technology Centers (http://www.astc.org/camp/adalaw.htm)

3. How large is the physical size of the print, audio, and video resource collection? Sufficient room needs to be allotted for the size and organization of the collection the center develops. Include space for users to sit and examine the materials. Local professionals who have expertise in these areas (librarians, for example) may be very useful as resources regarding the space and equipment necessary to adequately design the center.

4. How many people does the center intend to serve at any one time? One of the biggest challenges is developing a center with the capacity to serve large numbers. Once the center has identified the population it intends to serve, develop a plan for delivering service that includes a variety of methods, some of which may be off-site. Search for alternate methods of delivering services that do not require the physical presence of the user (for example, an Internet site that provides much of the career-related support needed by users).

In Florida, a unique partnership between the schools in two counties (Volusia and Flagler), a community college, and the local Workforce Development Boards resulted in the Career Connection Coach. The Career Connection Coach is a mobile career resource center equipped with the latest multi-media technology that provides individual career assessment, exploration, and planning opportunities.

While the coach serves a comparatively small number of students at any one time, it can serve a larger geographic area than any stationary center. Conveniently, it can go to the students rather than the students having to go to it. The area inside the coach has been carefully developed to provide computer workstations, and also meeting/non-computer work space. This is a very creative approach to addressing the needs of the users where they live.

5. *What different methods of delivery are anticipated? Is there a need for classrooms?* Space for workshops or other meetings? The method of delivering career information and counseling is coupled with the identified user population characteristics, the amount of space available, the staff strengths, and the goals of the center. It might also be valuable to consider providing center users with experiential workstations to experiment with tasks associated with different occupations.

Also consider the different learning styles that users bring to the center. For some users, written information may be enough while others might seek workshops and interactive classes to gather the information or assistance they need. Carefully consider the types of services the center plans to offer prior to designing the center because it is difficult to create classroom space once the layout has been completed.

6. *How much space is necessary to accommodate people and the technology (including computers, overheads, audio and video) utilized?* Provide space for users' computer workstations. Space on either side of a workstation should be free so that several users can view the computer at one time. In some cases this might also be a place for students and their parents to investigate and explore career information on the Internet, or for an adult to work on her or his resume.

If the center plans on offering workshops or classes, be sure to include adequate room space for that. Some centers use recessed screens for overheads or computer projectors that can transform a career center into a meeting room. Also consider using a lighting system with a dimmer switch to allow for image projection while providing enough light for workshop participants to write notes.

Again, if assessment is taking place at a center that also uses a lot of audio or video, consider designing the center in such a way that the two activities can occur at the same time. If that is not possible, note that as a challenge when it comes to scheduling activities in the center.

7. What can be done to make the career center aesthetically appealing and welcoming? Potential users must see the career center as a friendly environment in which they are free to browse and work at their own pace. Such an environment can be created by some simple decorating maneuvers. If you are starting from scratch or have the opportunity to redecorate existing facilities, choose paint and carpeting in warm, inviting colors. Lighting must be appropriate for reading and other tasks, but it should not be overbright or harsh. You might consider powerful individual reading lamps to complement softer overhead lighting. Furniture—especially chairs—should be comfortable and present a well-coordinated look. Every career center can arrange colorful, orderly displays of handouts, books, and other materials. Green plants, inexpensive and easy to care for, are good ways to combat even the most unwelcoming or utilitarian settings.

Finally, plan ahead for growth and expansion. Try to anticipate the needs of the community one year from now, even five years from now. Using the labor market information, will the community experience new growth or will many of the currently employed citizens lose their jobs? Develop a layout that can deal with short-term capacity overload, and prepare for long-term growth.

Equipment

Choosing the right equipment may depend on the type of center developed. Barbieri (1991) identified three different levels of career resource centers.

The first level center, or *core center,* offers basic reference material and a designated location for interactions between users and center staff or representatives from the community. Where space is at a premium, particularly in an academic setting, a core center can easily be established in a corner of an existing library. A core center must include tables, chairs, bookshelves, job board, and check-out facilities. It must also have a basic selection of books and materials from each of the three categories outlined in

Chapter Four, which is to say assessment tools, career and labor market information, and strategy-based references. Where reference materials are limited, the center can provide lists of resources that are available in nearby public libraries or elsewhere.

The second level center, or *expanded core center,* includes everything in the core center plus more resources connected to high technology. A VCR with a monitor is a simple and useful addition, as is a fax machine. A computer with a printer, CD-ROM drive, and Internet access is becoming a necessity and should be added to your center at this stage. However, the most complete and well-established career resources are still print-based, so take care to ensure that your expanded core center contains an expanded print section as well.

Barbieri (1991) described the third level as the *comprehensive center.* At this level, a center should facilitate individual and group activities, as well as provide career counseling staff for advice and technical support. It goes without saying that comprehensive centers should also update and expand their collections of print and electronic media.

Specific items, particularly reference materials, will differ among academic and adult career centers, but all centers should make provision for the entire career development process. Most career centers possess items from the following list. Your own checklist or shopping list will, of course, be determined by your budget and the needs assessment explored in Chapter Two.

- Bookshelves
- Bulletin boards
- Chairs
- Computers
- Computer printers
- Computer scanners
- Computer server
- Computer tables
- Copy machine
- Desks

- Disk storage facility
- Display shelves
- Fax machine
- File cabinets
- Job board
- Modem
- Monitor
- Overhead and screen
- Portable cart for VCR & monitor
- Registration/checkout station
- Room dividers
- Tables
- Telephone(s)
- Typewriter
- Typing table
- VCR & monitor
- Workstations

Consider carefully the medium most appropriate for the primary population served by the center. While there may be many options when it comes to videos, are they the most effective medium for the center's target audience? Longer videos in particular might not hold the audience's attention when compared to the fast connections of the Internet. Talk with other centers, or with organizations and schools that presently work with the target audience before purchasing materials that may be underutilized.

Technology

One of the most costly and challenging investments that career centers make is their computer system. To address the issue of rapid technological changes, it is important to develop a plan for how computer technology can assist users with the career development process. From that plan, decisions can be made regarding hardware and software. Often, technology plans "simply itemize what computers and software will be purchased, what will be networked and where the computers will be located. They seldom address how the technology will be used or how teachers [and staff] are to be trained" (Golden 1997).

Here are some guidelines for developing the plan (adapted from Golden 1997).

- List the hardware, software, and infrastructure that will be required and show how it all works together and with existing technologies.
- Explain how the technology will be integrated with other services, into school curricula, and into local educational agencies, and how it will enhance learning.
- Describe how the career center will ensure ongoing, sustained professional development for staff and users.
- Show which supporting resources—such as services, software, and print resources—will be acquired to ensure successful and effective use of technologies.
- Project the total cost of the technology to be acquired and related expenses needed to implement such a plan.
- Describe how the career center will involve the community in the plan's development.
- Describe a process for the ongoing evaluation, including how technology will affect career development and progress toward meeting center and user goals.

Staff often struggle with what equipment to purchase. Consult qualified and knowledgeable resources in management information systems, instructional technology, LAN managers, or computer technicians when developing the plan. A sample configuration for a computer (a PC in this case) might look like this:

- 300 MHz Pentium II Processor (MMX)
- Minimum 64 MB RAM (recommend 128 MB)
- 4 GB Hard Drive (minimum)
- 3.5" Disk Drive
- Minimum 12X CD-ROM (recommend 24X)
- 32 bit Soundblaster Card
- Video Card (4 MB)
- 100 MB Iomega ZIP Drive or 1 GB Jazz Drive (choose one to be the standard)
- 17" Color Monitor
- Keyboard
- Speakers

- Mouse
- 100 MB Ethernet Card (if not already included)
- Windows 95/NT 5.0

Also ask if the machine has any USB (Universal Serial Bus) connections. Such connections allow linkage to other types of video and audio devices. While this sample computer configuration might seem extravagant, it demonstrates the need to contemplate future needs when making computer-related purchases. Keep in mind that purchases today may have to last for many years and must be easy to upgrade and expand with the changes in technology.

Once the computers are in place, connecting to the Internet should be a consideration. Naturally, there are additional costs involved, most obviously for the external connection (the wide area networks connecting schools to each other and to the Internet) and the internal connection (local area networks that link computers within a given organization). Computers provide access to information and experiences unheard of in the past, but they come at a price greater than the bottom line on the order form—the costs of training staff and users and of ongoing operational support must be taken into account.

Summary

The physical components of your career center can be just as crucial to its success as the staff and materials inside it. The primary physical considerations are

- **Location.** The center should be near the main flow of traffic, away from noise and other distractions, and close to complementary facilities such as the offices of professional counselors.
- **Layout.** The layout and design must be suited to all the activities offered, accessible for users with a variety of disabilities, and large enough to accommodate all materials and anticipated visitors.
- **Equipment.** This includes everything from basic tables and chairs to optional fax machines and computer scanners.

- **Technology.** Costly but necessary, technological needs must be seriously considered and carefully planned for. Career centers might seek the advice of software and network specialists before committing to technology purchases.

Chapter 4

Critical Center Resources

by Don Schutt
with Pamela Hilleshiem-Setz and Shelley Drescher

Resources help career center users answer the three questions posed earlier: *Who am I? Where am I going?* and *How do I get there?* New resources are appearing on the market at a rapid pace. Most are exceptional in quality, but the consumer needs to clearly identify the needs of the center (as developed in Chapter Two) and then find resources that support the goals. Make a commitment to keep the resources current. This can be done by supplementing time-sensitive materials with alternate resources that are available over the Internet, for example. The many resources critical to a career center can be categorized into three basic areas: assessment tools, career and labor market information, and strategy-based references.

Assessment Tools

These tools help users learn more about themselves. The tasks that might be achieved with assessment tools include identifying individual strengths and weaknesses, fine tuning goals, determining academic skill levels, and conducting an interest and aptitude inventory. These tools range from formal psychometric instruments to informal resources such as portfolios and career-related games. In addition, they can measure different personality characteristics or areas.

It is vital to identify what it is you wish to find out and then seek an instrument that provides that information. For example, there are inventories that specifically measure aptitude (such as the Armed Services Vocational Aptitude Battery, or ASVAB), those that measure interests (such as the Self-Directed Search, or SDS), and others that measure values (the Temperament and Values Inventory). Kapes, Mastie, and Whitfield (1994a) pointed out that "before deciding to employ psychometric instruments for career assessment there is prerequisite contextual information the user needs to possess. This includes a knowledge of the instruments available for the intended use, access to sources of good information about the available instruments and awareness of the various legal, ethical and social considerations that impact the career assessment process." An example of a resource that can increase knowledge of a broad range of career-related instruments, published by the National Career Development Association, is *A Counselor's Guide to Career Assessment Instruments* (Kapes, Mastie, and Whitfield 1994b).

To select an instrument, Mehrens (1994) recommended using this outline:

1. State your purpose for testing
2. Describe the group that will be tested (e.g., age or grade)
3. Name of test
4. Author(s)
5. Publisher
6. Copyright date(s)
7. Purpose and recommended use as stated in the manual
8. Grade/age levels for which the instrument was constructed
9. Forms: Are equivalent forms available? What evidence is presented on the equivalence of the forms?
10. Format: comment on legibility, attractiveness, and convenience
11. Cost
12. Content of test and types of items
13. Administration and timing requirements
14. Scoring processes available (e.g., machine scoring)
15. Types of derived scores available
16. Types and quality of norms
17. Adequacy of reliability evidence presented in the manual
18. Validity evidence
19. General quality of administrative, interpretive and technical manuals
20. Comments about the instrument by outside reviewers
(Mehrens 1994)

In addition, consider these questions when selecting assessments:

- Is the reading level at the level of the intended users?
- Is the instrument published in languages other than English?
- Are there alternate formats for visually impaired users?
- Are the measures timed (and if so, do the norms also report any differences for users with disabilities who might need additional time)?
- Does your staff have the competence and training needed to ethically administer and interpret the results?

Another source of information on assessments is the National Occupational Information Coordinating Committee (NOICC) and its counterpart State Occupational Information Coordinating Committee (SOICC) networks. Typically, SOICCs work in three areas: career development, information delivery, and in training and technical support. In terms of assessment, some SOICCs have developed customized assessment instruments that are integrated into the Career Information Delivery System (CIDS) for the state. If your SOICC has not developed instruments, they may be able to refer career centers to the appropriate organization or resources in your area. Generally, the NOICC and the various SOICCs offer both print and electronic resources.

Examples of frequently used career-related computer software programs that offer a combination of assessment tools with career and labor market data include

- CareerExplorer (JIST Works, 720 North Park Avenue, Indianapolis, IN 46202, http://www.jist.com)
- CHOICES (CAREERWARE, ISM Information Systems Management Inc., 38465 NYS RT 12, P. O. Box 129, Clayton, NY 13624, http://www.careerware.com/)
- COIN Career Guidance System (COIN Educational Products, 3361 Executive Parkway, Suite 302, Toledo, OH 43606, http://www.coinep.com/)
- Discover (ACT, Educational Services Division, P.O. Box 168, Iowa City, IA 52243-0168, http://www.act.org/discover/)

- GIS—Guidance Information System (Guidance Customer Service, Riverside Publishing, 425 Spring Lake Drive, Itasca, IL 60143-2079, http://www.riverpub.com/)
- Magellan (Valpar International Corp., P. O. Box 5767, Tucson, AZ 85703-5797, http://biz.rtd.com/valpar)
- Mike Farr's Get a Job Workshop (JIST Works, 720 North Park Avenue, Indianapolis, IN 46202, http://www.jist.com)
- SIGI Plus (SIGI PLUS Program, Educational Testing Service, Princeton, NJ 08541, http://www.ets.org/sigi/)

There are also many print resources that have been used as informal assessments assisting in the career development process, including

- Center on Education and Work, University of Wisconsin-Madison. 1995. *STW self-assessment checklist.* Madison, WI: Center on Education and Work, University of Wisconsin-Madison.
- Hood, A. B., and Johnson, R. W. 1997. *Assessment in counseling: A guide to the use of psychological assessment procedures.* 2d ed. Alexandria, VA: American Counseling Association.
- Vernon, A. 1993. *Developmental assessment and intervention with children and adolescents.* Alexandria, VA: American Counseling Association.
- *What Color Is Your Parachute?* 1998. Berkeley, CA: Ten Speed Press.
- Zunker, V. G. 1990. *Using assessment results for career development.* 3d ed. Pacific Grove, CA: Brooks/Cole Publishing Co.

Regardless of the assessment instrument used, it is important to establish why and how the instrument was selected; which staff has the training necessary to administer, score, and interpret the instrument; and how the results will be communicated to the client.

Career and Labor Market Information

Complete, accurate, and timely information is critical as individuals make career decisions and form career plans. Career and labor market information responds to the question, *Where am I going?* As DeYoung (1998) noted, "career centers typically unify many functions such as intake, assessment, case management, employer services, and inter-agency planning." Career and labor market information can assist center users by offering opportunities for "career awareness, job and career counseling, training and educational referrals, job search assistance, literacy services, and occupational training." Career center users should be able to locate and use occupational information in making career decisions and developing their career plans. The occupational data that should be available to all users includes

- duties and nature of work,
- work setting and conditions,
- preparation required,
- special requirements or considerations (bonafide physical requirements, licenses, certifications, personal criteria, social or psychological factors, etc.),
- methods of entry,
- earnings and other benefits,
- usual advancement possibilities,
- employment outlook,
- opportunities for experience and exploration,
- related occupations, and
- sources of additional information.

(National Career Development Association 1994)

Career (or occupational) information is valuable to the user who is looking for information on employment trends, qualifications of employment, job descriptions related to a variety of occupations, and specific career or job openings. "It also consists of personal/social, educational and occupational information emphasizing individual characteristics, attributes, skills, knowledge, interests, values and aptitudes. This information is generally used by career decision makers and career guidance professionals to discover and explore occupational opportunities, related educational programs of study and training, the institutions that offer the programs, and other related information" (Ettinger 1996b). Career information assists users in picturing the work tasks and work environment by providing occupational descriptions. An example is a book or video focused on career biographies. Typically, it supplements the individual's perceptions of an occupation with the realities and allows for comparisons between occupations by providing the same data for each occupation or job. It can also be used to identify how one enters or advances in an occupational area, and the education/training necessary for success.

Labor market information is helpful to individuals who are looking for or exploring employment in a specific field or are interested in general job opportunities in a given geographic area. It is "data about workers, jobs, industries and employers including employment, demographic and economic data. It is generally used by administrators, planners, information analysts, policy makers, employers, and job seekers" (Ettinger 1996b). By reviewing the trends and outlooks for occupations, users can challenge misconceptions regarding areas where occupations are growing or shrinking. Labor market information also contributes to the picture users have of occupations as the industry or business data offers an idea of what is produced in any given industry.

Together, career and labor market information are used to gather background data regarding occupations, choose occupations, change work settings, or search for opportunities in specific geographic areas. In terms of computer software, the programs listed earlier also provide occupational and/or career information. A short list of print reference tools that should be considered include:

- Dunbar, R. E. 1992. *Guide to military careers.* Danbury, CT: Franklin Watts.
- *Encyclopedia of Careers and Vocational Guidance.* 1997. 10th ed. Chicago: Ferguson Publishing Co.
- Maze, M., and Mayall, D. 1995. *The enhanced guide for occupational exploration.* Rev. ed. Indianapolis, IN: JIST Works.

- Office of Management and Budget, Executive Office of the President. 1993. *Standard industrial classification manual.* Washington, DC: U.S. Government Printing Office.
- U.S. Department of Defense. 1997. *America's top military careers: The official guide to occupations in the armed forces.* 2d ed. Washington, DC: U.S. Government Printing Office.
- U.S. Department of Labor and Bureau of Labor Statistics. 1998. *Occupational outlook handbook 1998-99 edition.* Washington, DC: U.S. Government Printing Office.
- U.S. Department of Labor, Employment and Training Administration. 1991. *Dictionary of occupational titles.* 4th ed. Washington, DC: U.S. Government Printing Office. Also available on-line at: http://204.245.136.2/libdot.htm.

In addition to the tools listed in the previous section, there are other computer software programs that provide career and labor market information. These are just a few examples:

- *Career & College QUEST* (Peterson's, Publishing Group, 202 Carnegie Center, P. O. Box 2123, Princeton, NJ 08542-2123, http://www.petersons.com)
- *Career Information System* (National Career Information System, 1177 Pearl Street, Suite 200, Eugene, OR 97401)
- *Electronic Enhanced Dictionary of Occupational Titles* (JIST Works, 720 North Park Avenue, Indianapolis, IN 46202, http://www.jist.com)
- *Encyclopedia of Careers and Vocational Guidance on CD-ROM* (Ferguson Publishing, 200 West Madison Street, Suite 300, Chicago, IL 60606, http://www.fergpubco.com)
- *The O*NET Dictionary of Occupational Titles* (JIST Works, 720 North Park Avenue, Indianapolis, IN 46202, http://www.jist.com)
- *Peterson's Graduate Database (GradSearch)* (Peterson's, Publishing Group, 202 Carnegie Center, P. O. Box 2123, Princeton, NJ 08542-2123, http://www.petersons.com)
- *Young Person's Electronic Occupational Outlook Handbook* (JIST Works, 720 North Park Avenue, Indianapolis, IN 46202, http://www.jist.com)

In addition to the NOICC and SOICCs mentioned above, many publishing companies and distributors currently publish quality career-related materials. New materials are appearing constantly. Even though many of the materials that the career center purchases will likely come from for-profit publishers and educational material distributors, do not overlook alternate suppliers, including the American Vocational Association; the National Career Development Association; the National School-to-Work Office; the American School Counselor Association; the Department of Labor; the military; community surveys; Chambers of Commerce; labor unions; newspapers and magazines for time-sensitive information; corporations; federal, state, and local government printing offices; other professional and trade organizations; and colleges and universities.

There are also a number of resources that provide national data that can be accessed via the Internet. One is the Bureau of Labor Statistics (BLS) (http://stats.bls.gov/infohome.htm), the national statistical agency responsible for collecting, processing, analyzing, and disseminating statistical data to the public. As their home page states, "BLS data must satisfy a number of criteria, including relevance to current social and economic issues, timeliness in reflecting today's rapidly changing economic conditions, accuracy and consistently high statistical quality, and impartiality in both subject matter and presentation." The BLS has developed user friendly pages geared to draw in interest from a number of different populations.

One project currently in development at the national level is the O*NET (http://www.doleta.gov/programs/onet/). This is the Occupational Information Network, designed to replace the *Dictionary of Occupational Titles (DOT)*. The O*NET database, according to its Website, "identifies, defines, and describes the comprehensive elements of job performance in the changing world of work. It contains hundreds of information units on job requirements, worker attributes, and the content and context of work, capturing what people do as functions of their roles within organizations. By examining and measuring the process of work, O*NET data allow users to profile similarities and differences across occupations and anticipate skill changes now and into the

21st century." The actual database structures information into six categories: worker requirements, experience requirements, occupational requirements, occupation specifics, occupation characteristics, and worker characteristics. Additional Internet sites that might be of interest include FedStats (http://www.fedstats.gov/), the U.S. Census Bureau (http://www.census.gov/), and the Bureau of Economic Analysis (http://www.bea.doc.gov/).

Strategy-Based References

These resources assist the career center user with the development of resumes (paper and electronic formats), provide tips on interviewing, strategies for approaching businesses, and methods for interview follow-up. In other words, these resources address the question, *How do I get there?* Topics include

- developing workplace skills,
- positive work habits,
- test preparation materials (SAT, ACT, ASVAB, etc.),
- scholarship and financial aid information,
- college materials,
- job seeking materials,
- cover letters,
- resume writing,
- interviewing,
- getting a job and keeping it,
- recruitment literature, and
- military materials.

Some of these resources might include a combination of self-assessment, career and labor market information, and strategy-based references. The combination demonstrates how the information can be integrated into an individual's planning process. There are innumerable sources in this category, including

- Farr, J. M. 1994. *Getting the job you really want.* Indianapolis, IN: JIST Works.
- Jandt, F. E., and Nemnich, M. B. 1996. *Using the Internet and the World Wide Web in your job search.* Indianapolis, IN: JIST Works.

- Krannich, C., and Krannich, R. L. 1997. *Interview for success.* 7th ed. Manassas, VA: Impact.
- Ludden, L. 1997. *Job savvy: How to be a success at work.* 2d ed. Indianapolis, IN: JIST Works.
- Oakes, B. 1998. *Career exploration on the Internet.* Chicago: Ferguson Publishing Co.
- Weddle, P. D. 1994. *Electronic resumes for the new job market.* Manassas, VA: Impact.

Evaluating Materials

This section considers strategies for evaluating all materials for bias and stereotyping, and then brief, specific evaluations for career-related print, video, and software. The last three sections draw on the National Career Development Association (1994) guidelines for reviewing media. Printed guidelines and evaluation forms are available from the NCDA online at http://ncda.org/ or at 5999 Stevenson Avenue, Alexandria, VA 22304, 703-823-9800.

Also consider networking with other career centers, subscribing to a publication on career development, being involved in a chat-group related to career centers, passing on names of excellent texts, video, software and Websites, and developing display areas that focus on resources demonstrating positive career development methods for all individuals.

Bias and Stereotyping

It is important to preview all materials and resources before purchasing them for your career center. Many companies allow potential buyers to review their materials before purchasing. This gives you the opportunity to see if the name of the material and the contents are aligned. Careful screening of print, video, and software materials is necessary in order to expand clients' horizons with respect to job opportunities, to help career center users anticipate and deal with bias and discrimination on the job, and to provide them with information on equal employment opportunities. It is critical to help all career center participants understand, think about, and prepare for a future characterized by change and diversity, especially in female and male life roles, relationships, and careers.

There are several general guidelines that can help you with the evaluation of bias in career planning materials. The questions that follow apply equally to print and nonprint materials, in terms of the language, graphics, and the visual representations used. If you answer "no" to any of the questions below, bias, discrimination, and/or stereotyping may be present. It then becomes necessary to further analyze and review the materials, replacing them if necessary. If replacement is not an option, consider developing reference or supplemental material and discuss it with the user.

The following questions can be used as guidelines for rooting out bias in your career center resources:

1. Are occupations shown as open to all individuals regardless of race, sex, religion, creed, parental or marital status, sexual orientation, or physical, mental, emotional, and learning disability?
2. Are gender-free terms used in general (*people* or *humankind* instead of *man* or *mankind*)?
3. Are gender-free titles used to describe occupations (*firefighter* instead of *fireman, postal carrier* instead of *mailman*)?
4. Do females and males appear in approximately the same number?
5. Are males and females depicted in occupations currently dominated by the opposite sex (or are men shown in traditionally masculine careers and/or women in traditionally feminine careers)?
6. Are males and females portrayed in both active and passive roles in approximately the same number (or are men shown more often in active postures with women predominantly depicted as helpers, watching or sitting)?
7. Are various races and ethnic groups represented throughout the resource in a balanced fashion?
8. If references are made to family responsibilities, are the responsibilities shared between the sexes (or is a woman's

responsibility to raise a family while a man's responsibility is to be the economic provider)?

9. Are minority and nonminority, males and females, pictured equally in varied levels of occupational status and responsibility?

10. Do illustrations of people include a variety of body types and evidence of handicaps?

11. Is written reference made to physical appearance only when there is a genuine need for it?

12. After reviewing the material, do you come away with a sense that career opportunities are not limited by gender, race, or handicaps?

(Adapted from National Organization for Women 1972)

One strategy for preparing staff to confront issues of bias is to review select materials as a group, with each staff member using the guidelines, and then discussing the results together. In this way you provide a format for training staff in expectations regarding acceptable and unacceptable materials while increasing awareness beyond the confines of the media.

Using the questions above as guidelines will help all staff in the career center

- develop awareness about screening resources before sharing them with the general public;
- teach everyone to analyze the information they are receiving;
- help users become aware of the ways that idioms, expressions, and gender-bias language are used to discriminate; and
- provide the viewer with an opportunity to modify language or illustrations that appear biased.

Another method for ensuring that materials are evaluated to avoid stereotyping and bias is to always have a trained "career advocate" on staff. This individual provides a critical eye and can teach others to look for discriminatory information.

Career and Occupational Information Literature

The key to evaluating printed career and occupational literature information is ensuring that specific kinds of information are made explicit in the text. At a basic level, you should evaluate all literature by date of publication (is it still current?), credits and sources listed (are they unbiased and trustworthy?), format and vocabulary (are they appropriate and useful to the target audience?). The NCDA guidelines also say that occupational information should be evaluated on its inclusion of

1. duties and nature of the work,
2. work setting and conditions,
3. preparation required,
4. special requirements or considerations (including licensing requirements and bonafide physical requirements),
5. methods of entry,
6. earnings and other benefits,
7. usual advancement possibilities,
8. employment outlook,
9. opportunities for experience and exploration,
10. related occupations, and
11. sources of additional information.

Video Career Media

The NCDA guidelines for video career media deals with the objectives, concepts, and information portrayed in the video and the impact on the audience. In addition, they focus on both the content and the process. The guidelines include

1. early presentation of intent (purpose of video must be obvious early in the video),
2. integrity of title (must accurately reflect the content or purpose),
3. free from extraneous (non-career-related) material (content must be organized to fulfill stated objectives),
4. accurate and adequate presentation of concepts and information (must be portrayed and illustrated in a manner appropriate for the intended audience), and

5. simulates transition from passive to active response (must motivate audience toward appropriate behavioral response).

Career Software

The NCDA software guidelines focus on both the description of the software and the evaluation criteria. As to the description of the software, one should determine its objectives, how it is applicable to career development, who it is appropriate for, and what skills are prerequisite for using the software. The NCDA further suggests that users also consider the following five aspects of a software program as part of their evaluation:

1. Information in the program
2. Career development process
3. User interaction
4. Technical aspects of the software and materials
5. Support services

Organizing Materials

There are a number of different methods for organizing materials. The one you choose will depend upon your audience, your collection of materials, and the time and staff available to learn and implement the system. In addition to the methods listed here, you may want to create your own or adapt an established method to the particular needs of your career center.

- Academic Subject Classification (school subject area)
- Alphabetical
- Ann Roe's Two-Dimensional Occupational Classification Scheme (occupational titles on one level according to worker activities and the other level focusing on job stratification according to level of responsibility)
- Bennet Occupations Filing Plan and Bibliography (based on the field-of-work coding in the DOT)
- Categories (like self-understanding, college and university information, state CIDS, etc.)

- Chronicle Guidance Publication Plan (also use DOT and arranged under ten headings and subdivided into occupational fields)
- Dewey Decimal System (familiar and used by many libraries)
- DOT Occupational Titles Classification
- Holland Occupational Organization System (based on his six work environments and six interest areas)

(McDaniels and Gysbers 1992)

Summary

The three basic types of resources essential to a career center are assessment tools, career and labor market information, and strategy-based resources. Examples include:

Assessment Tools

- Tests measuring aptitudes (ASVAB), interests (SDS), and values (TVI)
- Computer software (CareerExplorer, SIGI Plus)
- Books and other print resources (*What Color Is Your Parachute?, Life Work Career Portfolio*)

Career and Labor Market Information

- Computer software (*Career & College QUEST, Encyclopedia of Careers and Vocational Guidance*)
- Books and other print resources (*Occupational Outlook Handbook, Dictionary of Occupational Titles*)
- Internet databases (Bureau of Labor Statistics, O*NET Occupational Information Network)

Strategy-Based Resources

- College and other postsecondary education materials
- Scholarship and financial aid information
- Instruments to improve such skills as interviewing and writing resumes

Prior to purchase, all of the above resources should be evaluated for bias and stereotyping. It is also wise to examine materials for such problems as the inclusion of non-career-related or extraneous information.

Possible methods of organizing the various resources within a career center include alphabetization, color coding, the Dewey Decimal System, and the DOT Occupational Titles Classification.

Chapter 5

Personnel, Administration, and Management

by Don Schutt

There are several approaches to managing the career center. A strong organizational structure is necessary to enable the delivery of the program processes. The framework suggested by NOICC (1995) to guide the development of comprehensive career development programs in schools also applies to the development of career centers that provide support for lifelong career development. The five components of the framework are

1. Leadership: A counselor or career development specialist who is supported by a staff dedicated to improving career development opportunities for users.
2. Management: Top-level staff organizing program planning, clarifying staff roles and responsibilities, securing resources, monitoring program delivery, and revising the program.
3. Personnel: Other staff, community resource persons, paraprofessionals, and volunteers who can help serve the wide range of career development needs through direct involvement or linkages with other organizations.
4. Facilities: Adequate space, materials, and equipment that ensure the delivery of career guidance and counseling services.
5. Resources: The funds required to purchase materials, equipment, and other items needed to implement a career guidance and counseling program.

This chapter considers who should be involved in the development (from external advisory groups to staff) and operation of the center, staff training suggestions, and budget considerations.

Development and Operation

The Advisory Group

Developing a strong advisory group allows the center to connect with and also take advantage of the resources existing in the community. The advisory group should comprise a diverse representation of career center stakeholders who have a strong interest in seeing the center succeed. Find representatives from the following groups:

- business, industry, trade, or union representatives (maybe from the local chamber of commerce or manufacturers association);
- community leaders (someone from the mayor's office, city or county board, local non-profit leaders, or key religious figures);
- community members (from the population the center intends to serve);
- K-12 representatives (local school-to-work coordinator, school counselors, teachers, principals);
- past users of the career center (or of other career centers in the area);
- postsecondary representatives (community colleges, two-year and four-year college representatives);
- potential users (draw on people representing the target audiences);
- state government representatives (from the State Occupational Information Coordinating Committee office, the state department of public instruction or education, or the governor's office); and
- technology experts to guide the development of the career center information system.

In addition, if the career center is in a school, consider selecting parents, teachers, school counselors, and students to participate in developing and advising the center. The creation and utilization of an advisory group helps to develop strong community relations, opens communication channels, provides additional insights into selection criteria for program staff and materials, assists in evaluating the program, and expands the pool of individuals generating marketing strategies.

As an advisory group is identified and organized, it is important to be very clear about the roles and expectations of the members of the advisory group. More specifically, if the group is to provide suggestions or recommendations rather than make final decisions, be certain that the parameters of the decision-making process are clear. It is also helpful to orient members to the current career center (especially if they are entering midstream or if some of the decisions have already been made). Be open to the advice of the advisory group and avoid responses that appear defensive. If an advisory group is formed, the center has already accepted that the individuals in the group have experiences or perspectives that are important to the success of the center—draw on that information and use it to fully develop the services and programs at the center.

Once the group is identified and they have accepted the advisory group appointment, it is useful to provide an orientation to the program. Conducting a periodic review of the effectiveness of the advisory committee is also a useful process. As mentioned in previous chapters, the timing of this review should be decided in the center's continuous planning and improvement process. To gauge the effectiveness of the advisory committee, career centers should ask questions such as these:

Does the advisory committee . . .

> Represent a cross-section of the community?
> Assist in long-range and short-range planning?
> ●Establish priorities and develop objectives?
> ●Locate and support funding efforts?
> ●Coordinate utilization of community resources?
> ●Review and assess career center activities and recommend improvements?
> ●Assist in the center evaluation process?
> Communicate improvement information back to its constituents?
> Communicate information about the center to the media?

- Through newsletters?
- Through personal communication with constituencies?
- Through press releases?
- Through public meetings?
- Through reports?
- Through television, radio, Internet communications?

Work together effectively?

- Are meetings scheduled when necessary?
- Is attendance recorded?
- Is there a written agenda distributed?
- Are they a sounding board for new ideas?
- Are other opinions sought and heard?
- Are minutes recorded?

Taking time to create and evaluate the advisory group is valuable during program development as well as during program review. When advisory groups are utilized to the fullest potential, they can be a central source for the dissemination of information to stakeholders, the community, and potential career center users.

Staffing the Center

The process of identifying staff positions is directly connected to the mission and location of the center, space available, funding sources, services offered, and delivery methods. If the career center is in a middle school, the staff may focus more on integrating career development into the school curriculum, so a curriculum specialist might be more valuable than another position. Likewise, if the physical capacity of the center cannot provide enough room for the materials, a large staff might initially be inefficient. These complexities aside, a skeleton career center staff includes

- a manager/coordinator/director,
- professional counselors,
- professional librarians and information specialists,
- technology experts,
- paraprofessionals (might include support staff),
- volunteers,
- students, or
- some combination of these different employees.

The size of the staff and their individual duties will depend in a large part on how the center operates and how much financial support is available for staff. Career center staff face many challenges: "Staff in contemporary career centers not only must perform their own work, but also must coordinate and mobilize the efforts of dozens of partners seeking similar service goals—academic departments, external agencies, student clubs, campus unions, local businesses, other student service departments, government offices, plus others" (Casella 1990). Each of the staff positions contributes something different to the career center.

MANAGER/COORDINATOR/DIRECTOR

The person in this leadership and management position must have a strong understanding of the field of career development, as well as the components that are critical to developing and supporting comprehensive career development programs, and insights into successful management processes. Experience writing grants or soliciting funding would be additional desirable skills. Lastly, the manager should be competent in using technology, or at least have enough understanding of technology and systems to manage the use and future needs of technology in the career center.

The tasks of a manager/coordinator/director include: supervising staff, managing the day-to-day operations, searching for financial resources (when needed), developing collaborative partnerships with other organizations including schools and business/industry, and directing the continuous planning and improvement process guided by the mission and vision of the center. Here is a detailed sample job description for the Director of the Career Resource and Assessment Center at Grand Rapids (MI) Community College:

TITLE OF POSITION

Director of the Career Resource and Assessment Center (CRAC)

Classification: Faculty

71

MAJOR JOB RESPONSIBILITIES

1. Directly responsible to the Dean of Student Services
2. Responsible for the organization and administration of the CRAC
3. Administration and/or supervision of the center's testing services

ESSENTIAL FUNCTIONS

1. Supervising and/or conducting career counseling and test interpretations for individuals and small groups
2. Providing career consultation and referral services
3. Providing in-service, training, and supervision of CRAC personnel
4. Previewing, evaluating, and purchasing career and testing materials
5. Maintaining a familiarity with test manuals, booklets, procedures, and instructions of major tests and surveys administered by the CRAC
6. Developing and maintaining career files and library
7. Providing/displaying and disseminating information related to career/occupational and social/personal development
8. Revising, updating, and whenever necessary developing operational materials
9. Facilitating and/or conducting career-related seminars, workshops, classroom presentations, etc.
10. Communicating to staff, students, and/or the community information related to services offered, new materials available, upcoming career-related activities, etc.
11. Other duties as assigned by the Dean

REQUIREMENTS

1. Possess at least a master's degree in guidance and counseling, psychology, or equivalent
2. Possess the ability to interpret/analyze, test data of all types (career, personality, aptitude, intelligence, ability, achievement, and placement)
3. Be able to work effectively with people of differing ages, ethnic backgrounds, and gender

4. Be willing to work flexible hours
5. Possess a high energy level along with enthusiasm and a genuine interest in assisting individuals in planning their career development

A disadvantage to having a manager/director is cost. Many centers that originated in a different form, like a library or counseling office, cannot afford a manager/director. Center staff in this situation often divide the managerial tasks among themselves. For most career centers, the most effective approach is to hire a manager/coordinator/director.

PROFESSIONAL COUNSELOR(S)

If the center plans to offer career counseling, it is important that competent, professionally trained and licensed counselors are available to provide the service. How do you differentiate between career advising and career counseling? Rayman described career advising as "brief immediate assistance provided by paraprofessional staff with an emphasis on information giving and receiving. He further characterized individual career counseling as "the establishment of a therapeutic relationship between a professionally trained and skill certified career counselor and a client involving significant psychological content, formal assessment and interpretation, teaching, coaching, and information giving in the context of a one-to-one relationship" (Rayman 1996).

There are three reasons why professional counselors are vital to a career center:

1. It may be that the services the center is preparing to offer fall somewhere between these two areas (of career advising and career counseling), which is why having appropriately trained counselors available to make those decisions are critical to center functioning.
2. It is also not uncommon for individuals seeking career assistance to find that while they want to work on career decision-making, other life expectations or situations complicate that opportunity or ability to make the critical decisions. Counselors trained in career development can

help individuals identify career-related issues and conflicting life-related issues.
3. Most counselors have received training in the area of career development and assessment.

What criteria can you use to find professional counselors? There is a national organization that connects with many states to identify and certify counselors called the National Board for Certified Counselors (NBCC), located at: http://www.nbcc.org/, by phone at 336-547-0607, or by mail: National Board for Certified Counselors, Inc., 3 Terrace Way, Suite D, Greensboro, NC 27403-3660. That Internet site offers an opportunity to get a list of certified counselors in your area. A list of state credentialing boards can be found on the Internet at: http://www.nbcc.org/states/boards.htm

There is also an area of specialization in counseling certified through the NBCC called the National Certified Career Counselor (NCCC) program. The NCCC specialty credential attests to the educational background, knowledge, skills, and competencies of the specialist in the specific area of career counseling. More information can be found about this certification at the NBCC Website. For both NCCCs and National Certified Counselors, there are requirements for certification including work experience, course work, professional assessments, and examination. In order to remain certified, these counselors must also participate in continuing education.

As with managers/coordinators/directors, one disadvantage to having professional counselors is salary costs.

PROFESSIONAL LIBRARIAN OR INFORMATION SPECIALIST
Career centers sometimes struggle early on to develop a systematic method for organizing and displaying materials and resources. Professional librarians and information specialists are experts at organizing and cataloging materials. There are three strong reasons for considering professional librarians or information specialists:

1. "Librarians or information specialists are generally aware of the sources of material, how to secure them, classifica-

tion and filing systems, methods for displaying material, and procedures for the maintenance of the collection" (Brown and Brown 1990).

2. Many have experience organizing materials using technology. This knowledge increases the opportunities for moving the internal career center resources to the Internet and offering access to the career center after conventional office hours.

3. Often they are familiar with strategies for funding resources and may already have a budget for resources.

A strategy for identifying well-trained library staff is to look for graduates from accredited library and information studies masters programs. One source of valuable information in this area is the American Library Association, which maintains a list of accredited master's degree programs online at http://www.ala.org

One drawback is that a librarian's background in career development may be limited, so much of his or her time would be focused on the organizational tasks. If cost is a factor, this could also be done as a short-term appointment to start up the center's materials; the librarian may then return periodically as a consultant.

TECHNOLOGY EXPERTS

The need for staff with expertise in technology-related areas is easy to understand. One of the challenges that can occur is hiring staff with more than one area of expertise (like an information specialist who is also a Webmaster). The challenge becomes balancing immediate duties with the center's long-term goals. The other challenge is keeping a computer-savvy counselor current with new and increasingly fast changes in technology while also allowing him or her to assist users in career decisions.

As the center approaches hiring technology experts, consider which areas are most important. Following are a few questions to ponder.

- Who will troubleshoot the computer problems on the computers the center currently owns?
- Who will load the career-related software?
- Who will train the staff and users on the software?

- Are the computers networked? Who will manage that network?
- Will your experts need to have technical training in repairing computers?
- Are you planning to have a complicated Internet site that will require continuous updating? Will they need to know how to write HTML language, Common Gateway Interface (CGI) scripts, Java scripts, or place pictures on the site? (If these are unfamiliar terms, it is even more important to have someone skilled in technology on staff.)
- Will they also be editing the Internet site? Do they have editing skills?
- Will users need to register for activities and can that occur through a Website?
- Are you planning to keep a database of all users for advertising upcoming events? Do your experts have database experience?
- Will resources be kept in an electronic database?
- Will your experts need to monitor listservs and online discussion rooms related to career development?
- Will they be responsible for an internal email system or intranet?
- Will technology be used to deliver workshops and presentations?

Three main areas which necessitate technology are administering the network or computer system (possibly including the purchase of individual and system hardware), directing the implementation of an Internet site, and managing complex databases. The staff responsible for each area should have practical experience working among all three areas.

This discussion demonstrates the need for advisory group members with expertise in technology. They might even assist in the hiring process for this position. When hiring for technology positions, be sure to have the candidates provide samples of their work. It might be difficult to understand how someone created a unique feature on a Web page, but personally using the feature provides managers with insight into the skill and ability levels of potential staff members.

The challenge related to technology positions is in hiring skilled technology staff and then meeting the salary needs. One alternative can be outsourcing technology demands, although this often costs a great deal more, and centers may have less control over the outcome.

PARAPROFESSIONALS AND VOLUNTEERS

These two groups have been combined as the tasks they undertake are similar in many ways. The daily tasks necessary for operating a career center might include clerical work such as filing, responding to correspondence, answering phones, organizing materials, scheduling appointments for other center staff, or coordinating the logistics for upcoming activities. It might also include orienting new users to the resources and services provided by the center, along with answering questions. It is important that paraprofessionals and volunteers are not asked to take on tasks or roles for which they are not prepared (such as career counseling).

When recruiting paraprofessionals and volunteers, consider past center users, retirees, students, or parents. Once hired, plan orientation and follow-up training sessions for the staff. Provide regular (once every three months if possible) performance feedback to volunteers and paraprofessional staff.

Deciding whom to enlist to complete the tasks in the career centers means finding a balance between cost and success. Often, volunteers are willing to offer shorter periods of available times than are paid staff, who may want half-time or full-time positions. The number of staff may affect the time that managers/coordinators/directors need to spend doing supervision and training. A center that is open five days a week and staffed by volunteers might require eight to ten individuals to cover the hours of business. A center staffed by paraprofessionals, more costly than volunteers, may only have one to two individuals to cover the same hours. A system combining paraprofessionals and volunteers might be more ideal, providing continuity with lower costs.

STAFFING SUMMARY

The composition of the staff is an important component of the center. These recommendations summarize key points to consider:

- Make program development and partnership-building a significant part of a staff person's job description, especially during the start-up phase.
- Once a program or system is up and running, make sure there is someone on staff with enough time to manage partnership relations and to coordinate program improvement and development.
- Hire or designate a program coordinator.
- Make sure specialized programs have enough staff to ensure a low user-staff ratio.
- Accept higher caseloads in programs serving a wider range of users or employers, but do not go beyond the point where the caseloads can be managed effectively.
- Gear caseload size to user characteristics.
- Set staffing patterns to match the size and complexity of the program.
- Make sure staff have a combination of the qualities needed to ensure a successful program.

(Adapted from Hoffinger and Goldberg 1995)

Staff Training

Each of the staff positions listed above carries with it its own education and training requirements, but the common thread that connects them all is the need for ongoing training and development as a part of their work time. At a minimum, staff should receive training in the career development process and the role that their career center intends to play. This might include having staff create their own professional development plans using the existing resources in the center. This kind of knowledge of center resources is absolutely necessary for the staff, as are brief refresher courses on the center's policies and procedures.

A moderate level of ongoing staff training might include advanced skills in using the Internet for career development. Additionally, staff should explore the vast array of career development resources now available in many media, even if their own center does not yet own or use them. At this level, many national organizations—the National Career Development Association, the American School Counselor Association, etc.—and their state affiliates can provide more formalized training opportunities.

Ideally, staff would be trained in customer service and strategic planning as well as the areas mentioned above. As with many other aspects of planning and developing a career center, it is worthwhile to visit and work with other career centers in your area. This not only allows a sharing of ideas, but may also present opportunities to conduct the occasional joint training session.

Budget

Preparing a budget is an important task. The budget should be prepared in advance of requesting funding and be divided into two categories: one-time costs (or start-up costs) and an operating budget (Brown and Brown 1990; Hoffinger and Goldberg 1995; Workforce Development Center 1995).

- Start-up costs include: furniture, equipment (including computers and associated hardware), resource collections, site development costs (which might be remodeling, rent, or land purchase costs), and the initial salaries and expenses.
- Operating budget should include: salaries and fringe benefits, capital expenditures (cost of replacing, repairing or purchasing new equipment), costs for materials, advertising costs, office costs (such as postage, utilities, printing), professional development costs, and any costs that are imposed by fiscal agents acting on your behalf.

As the center prepares the initial budget, consider consulting with Service Corps of Retired Executives, which has offices in most larger cities (or contact them on the Internet at http://www.score.org/). SCORE offers free consultation with retired business professionals and online business counseling. This is a resource that few career centers consider, but it is often relied upon by individuals and groups starting up businesses (which a career center is). Brown and Brown (1990) suggested other resources as the center budget is developed:

- Remodeling: either the maintenance department of the organization or an outside contractor can provide estimates of these costs
- Salaries: check local and institutional salaries
- Furniture and equipment: check catalogs, office supply stores, audiovisual equipment vendors, etc.
- Core collection: contract other centers as well as publisher catalogs (which may also be online) to determine costs
- Other: estimate remaining costs on the basis of other operations within the organization

There is a wide variety of funding sources. Some centers are developed out of school counseling programs, where others have been funded by state job service agencies and still others from school-to-work funding. If the center developers have access to the Internet, these sites might be useful in identifying and preparing grant proposals:

- Educational Grants Page (links to other grant sites): http://www.uen.org/utahlink/train/manuals/urlindex/edugrants.html
- The Foundation Center Online (information on a variety of topics related to grant finding): http://fdncenter.org/index.html
- RAMS-FIE, Inc. (sources from all over the world): http://www.rams-fie.com/resource.htm; also check out their home page for software and services to ease the grant-seeking process: http://www.rams-fie.com/
- SRA Resource Guide (print sources for grant finding): http://ftp.rttonet.psu.edu/~sra/restrict/rguidetc.htm
- The Society of Research Administrators GRANTSWEB (a starting point for accessing grant-related information and resources on the Internet): http://web.fie.com/cws/sra/resource.htm

- Yahoo's grant page: http://www.yahoo.com/education/ financial_aid/grants/

If you do not have access to the Internet, contact a local library for assistance. Many of these institutions offer workshops and print information that can guide center developers through the process.

In general, when dealing with budget and funding issues:

- Recognize program staffing as central to overall program cost.
- Find ways to create efficiencies in staffing and to leverage other resources.
- Consider the cost implications of different organizational and staffing structures.
- Use strategies to lower net additional costs to schools and programs.
- Launch programs with enrollments high enough to justify the necessary investment in staff resources.

(Adapted from Hoffinger and Goldberg 1995)

Summary

When organizing the management of your career center, it is vital to consider several key components. Developing an advisory group from all sectors of the community can be a valuable first step toward carrying out these key tasks efficiently.

The importance of selecting and maintaining a suitable staff for your center can hardly be overstated. The staff at most career centers might include

- a manager, coordinator, or director;
- professional counselors;
- professional librarians or information specialists;
- technology experts; and/or
- paraprofessionals and volunteers.

The proper planning and execution of a budget is crucial to the effective management of every career center. The Internet and your local library can provide leads on possible sources of funding. Regardless of where you get your funding, you must budget for both start-up costs and operating expenses.

Chapter 6

Career Centers in Educational Settings

by Don Schutt

Career centers can serve as a hub in educational institutions around which career development activities occur. While the primary target audience is typically the students, the center should also serve as a resource center for staff including faculty, student services staff, and counselors. This is often accepted as a reality in high schools but not considered important in elementary schools, middle/junior high schools, and postsecondary institutions. Chapter One proposed that career development be considered as a process of answering the three critical questions, *Who am I?*, *Where am I going?*, and *How do I get there?* Schools can prepare students for resolving these lifelong questions by providing developmentally appropriate career-related experiences.

The role of the career center in schools, colleges, and universities is to offer practical and timely information and services to students, to support and increase the instructional capacity of the institution by serving as a resource to the faculty and staff, and to reinforce student progress as they create and implement career plans. This applies to career centers that are located in schools, colleges, and universities as well as those which are located outside of the physical boundaries of the campus but serve student populations.

When considering career development as a developmental progression, it is implied that each developmental stage builds on the previous stage. Therefore, teaching students the process of becoming aware of themselves and the workplace is a necessary preliminary step that leads to the exploration stage. A challenge arises when there is a gap between where schools might expect students to be developmentally and where they really are. It is not uncommon for career development to not be addressed until eighth grade. Essentially this means that the students must compress eight years of developmental career-related learning and skill building into a year or less (around eighth grade). This can result in students not being prepared to make the decisions that they need to make, such as choosing their high school courses. This lack of preparation is complicated by students lacking the personal and workplace information needed to make good decisions, so they might decide to attend a four-year college without regard to (or in place of) future planning. The National Career Development Guidelines can serve as a guide to individual goals at every educational and developmental level. Planning center programs to meet the competency needs identified in the Guidelines is one strategy for ensuring the comprehensive development of individuals.

How can career centers work with institutions at different educational levels? Generally, centers should work to educate students and faculty about their services, and to create center programs that support the expansion of career-related activities and experiences into the curriculum. These experiences contribute to students' career development in three essential ways:

- Teaching students the skills necessary to answer the three questions at times when they are developmentally prepared to learn and use the information
- Assisting faculty in identifying teaching points in existing curricula where the content can be used to teach students the process of connecting course material to the world of work
- Reinforcing the development of critical career development competency areas by asking students to apply their knowledge and skills to increasingly complex situations

The following four sections detail additional programming considerations for students at the different educational levels.

Elementary Schools

At the elementary level, career centers should work collaboratively with school faculty to teach students the processes of identifying interests and aptitudes, connecting skills with occupations, connecting learning and school subjects with the world of work, and finally how to use information for planning. More specifically, career centers and elementary schools could provide students with experiences though which students

- realize that understanding one's strengths, values, and preferences is the foundation for education and occupational choices;
- understand that it is possible to achieve future goals by planning and preparation in the present;
- achieve a sense of personal competence to choose and to meet the requirements of educational and occupational alternatives;
- consider the implications of change in one's self, in one's options, and in relation to the need for continuing education throughout life;
- understand the similarities between problem-solving skills and personal decision-making skills;
- develop an unbiased, nonstereotyped base of information on which to base later educational and occupational decisions;
- understand that schooling is made up of many opportunities to explore and prepare for life;
- recognize the relationships between academic skills— reading, writing, computation—and other subject matter and how these are used in future educational and work options;
- identify occupations in which people work with others, with ideas, or with things;
- consider the relationships between occupation, career, and lifestyle;
- describe the purposes that work serves for different people; and
- consider the importance of effective use of leisure time.

(Adapted from Herr 1976 as cited in Herr and Cramer 1996)

Career centers can expose students to occupations or jobs beyond that which their own life experiences might provide. This is particularly important for students who have life experiences that are limited by constraints like income level. An example of a program that a center might cosponsor in an elementary school is a "Careers in Uniform Day," where workers from occupations that demand the wearing of uniforms come to talk with students. The career center might organize the structure of the day's events and draw on its community contacts, while the school might provide the physical space, follow-up processing of the event, and lunch for the speakers. Through this event, students could increase their awareness of a variety of occupations that might connect with their interests.

Regardless of the specific methods they use, career centers at the elementary school level should

- Educate parents about the career development process so school staffs feel increased support for implementing career-related activities
- Work with school staff to increase their understanding of the vital role that they play in the career development process—many elementary level educators do not believe that they contribute to the process. Help them to see how skills like working with others is an important part of working later in life
- Provide educational opportunities for school staff to enhance their understanding of the complexities of the world of work and their connection to it
- Cosponsor developmentally appropriate educational events with schools
- Make connections between schools, businesses, industry and postsecondary institutions.

Often career development is not considered at the elementary level. For this reason, few examples of structured interventions by career centers exist in elementary schools.

Middle/Junior High Schools

Career centers can work with middle/junior high educators to provide experiences for students and for staff. Students at this level need to

- understand that achievement of one's goals in life is related to a positive attitude toward work and learning;
- learn how to use a career planning process by preparing an individual education/career plan for middle school and how to anticipate changes as a result of personal maturation and social needs;
- develop an awareness of the level of competency in academic areas needed to achieve career goals;
- understand how interests, work values, achievements, and abilities affect career choice;
- learn that nontraditional occupations offer expanded career opportunities; understand what employers expect of applicants and employees;
- learn about leisure and recreational activities that best fit personal needs and interests and contribute to personal satisfaction;
- understand personal qualities (e.g., dependability, punctuality, getting along with others) that are needed to secure and keep a job;
- know the sources of information about available jobs and how to complete a job application;
- know about training opportunities that will enhance employment potential;
- develop knowledge of the relationship between school subjects and future educational and occupational choices without regard for prejudice, bias, or stereotyping;
- be aware of alternative educational and vocational choices and the corresponding preparation for them;
- understand the challenges, adjustments, and advantages of nontraditional occupations;
- be aware of employment trends as they relate to training programs and employment opportunities; and
- be aware of the factors that impede performance and productivity in the workplace.

(From the Pennsylvania Department of Education as reported in Herr and Cramer 1996).

The types of experience that career centers might develop for students include job shadowing opportunities, career awareness fairs, and mentoring relationships with community businesses.

Career centers can also work with schools to guarantee that student career assessment results or interest inventory results are accurately interpreted and the information is used in a manner that is ethical and accurate. Career centers might support the school assessment process with worksheets that connect the assessment to center resources, and then connect the results of that process to student opportunities for greater exploration of the world of work (like information interviews).

Career centers can work collaboratively with school staff to seamlessly infuse career development into the curriculum. This might mean working with teachers to coordinate the content in a number of courses so that the result is students examining occupations in greater detail or from different perspectives. One example is teaching the *Diary of Anne Frank* at the same time that World War II history is taught. For history class, it might be the ideal time for the class to learn how the composition of the occupational structure shifts in a country during times of war. For English class, it might mean identifying possible occupational options for central characters based on interest inventories students complete as if they were that character. Timing these two curriculum pieces so that they run concurrently is one example of how subtle the infusion of career development might be in curriculum.

Career centers at the middle/junior high school level should

- continue to educate students, school staff, and parents about the career development process,
- publicize the career development resources available in the center to parents and school staff,
- teach students about the many strategies for accessing information and the connections between the information databases,
- work with students to increase skills in the areas of managing information and planning,
- support efforts to get students involved in workplace simulation activities or actual work sites, and
- guide students in the creation of a career development portfolio.

High Schools

At the high school level, career centers need to help students synthesize the information they have been gathering in the earlier stages of development. Unfortunately, many students are not involved in career development activities and many schools do not infuse career-related experiences into the curriculum. The result is that a number of students reach high school developmentally unprepared to make the decisions they now face.

Herr and Cramer (1996) offered several concerns that need to be addressed as students prepare for the transition from high school to their next destination. While this excerpt addresses primarily career guidance issues, understanding the challenge that high school students face equips career centers with valuable information around which programming can develop.

1. Because many students will complete their formal education with the senior high school and thereby terminate their opportunities for the systematic analysis and facilitation of their career development, efforts need to be undertaken to reach all students with career guidance opportunities and to help them develop and implement an individual career plan.
2. The major career guidance emphasis in senior high school needs to be on the specific and comprehensive planning of immediate, intermediate and future educational and occupational choices after high school. For many reasons, however, not all senior high school students will be ready for such planning. Many students will need intensive self-awareness or career awareness and exploration activities, either because they did not have such experiences in the junior high school or because they were not ready to profit from them at that time.
3. Owing to the nature of senior high school students and the diversity of their goals, career guidance in senior high school should include counseling and developmental guidance experiences dealing with study habits, human relations at work, career and educational planning, job search techniques, and job interview skills.

4. Decisions must be made about how career guidance and placement will correspond or differ in the senior high school. Will placement be seen as a process spanning the total senior high school period or an event primarily dealt with in the twelfth grade? Will counselors take sole responsibility for educational and occupational placement or will they share these elements with other persons (such as vocational teachers or employment service counselors) in the school and the community?

5. The senior high school student is confronted with internal and external pressures to make decisions and to pursue specific types of outcomes. Career guidance can help students deal effectively with these pressures.

6. The verbal and conceptual skills of high school students are more developed than those of junior high school students, permitting career guidance to proceed along multiple and complex dimensions.

7. Because the major combinations of possibilities following high school are reasonably clear—college, other postsecondary education, work, nonwork, military, or governmental service (such as VISTA, Action)—career guidance should help senior high students to consider the advantages and disadvantages of each.

Career centers at the high school level should

- teach students to consider themselves in terms that include not only what they know, but also what they can do;
- work with students to use their portfolios to develop career development plans that include answers to the who, where, and how questions; long-term goals; training and education necessary to obtain those goals; short-term goals (what can happen in the next year); and the identification of the pertinent decision points ahead (encouraging students to see that they have decisions);
- continue to educate students, parents, schools, and the rest of the community on career development as a lifelong concept; and

- assess student readiness (in other words, where they are developmentally in terms of career development), and provide experiences, direction, knowledge, and opportunities for students who are not prepared to increase their readiness to make effective, personally meaningful career plans.

What Is School-to-Work?

School-to-work is a new approach to education in America that prepares students for life beyond the classroom. It combines traditional academic learning with practical experiences in today's world of work.

In the early 1990s, Congress found that a disproportionately large number of high school students in the United States enter the workforce without adequate academic and entry-level occupational skills. Dropout rates and unemployment among youth are intolerably high. Workplaces face heightened international competition, increasing the demand for highly skilled labor. Yet the United States lacks an educational system that gives young people the knowledge, skills, abilities, and information they need to make a successful transition from school to career-oriented work or to further education and training.

These and other findings precipitated the School-to-Work Opportunities Act, enacted into federal legislation in 1994. The Act outlines a comprehensive education reform that offers opportunities for all students, including those from culturally, racially, and ethnically diverse backgrounds, disadvantaged youth, and the disabled. It promotes the creation of a high-quality transition system that helps students identify and navigate career paths. It encourages the use of workplaces as active learning environments, and other school-to-work activities, such as tech-prep education, career academies, cooperative education, youth apprenticeships, school-sponsored enterprises, and business-education agreements. The Act also provides venture capital to states and communities to underwrite the initial costs of planning and establishing statewide school-to-work systems.

According to the Act, a School-to-Work Opportunities Program must include a school-based learning component, a work-based learning component, and a connecting activities component.

The school-based learning component must include

1. Career awareness and career exploration and counseling beginning at the earliest possible age, but no later than the seventh grade.
2. Selection of a career major no later than the beginning of the eleventh grade.
3. A program of study that meets the academic standards the state sets for all students, including the standards established under the Goals 2000: Educate America Act. The program must also meet the requirements for postsecondary preparation and earning of a skills certificate.
4. A program of instruction and curriculum that integrates academic and vocational learning, and incorporates instruction in all aspects of an industry tied to a student's chosen career major.
5. Regularly scheduled evaluations to identify students' academic strengths and weaknesses, academic progress, workplace knowledge, goals, and the need for additional learning opportunities to master core academic and vocational skills.
6. Procedures to ease students' entry into and transfer between additional training or postsecondary education programs.

Work-based learning components must include

1. Work experience.
2. Job training and work experiences, coordinated with learning in school-based components, that are rele-

vant to career majors and lead to the award of skill certificates.

3. Workplace mentoring.
4. Instruction and activities in general workplace competencies, including positive work attitudes, employability, and participative skills.
5. Broad instruction, to the extent practicable, in all aspects of the industry.

The connecting activities component must include

1. Matching students with work-based learning opportunities of employers.
2. School site mentors to liaise among students, employers, teachers, school administrators, and parents.
3. Technical assistance and services to employers.
4. Assistance to schools and employers for integrating school-based and work-based learning
5. Encouraging the active participation of employers, in cooperation with local education officials.
6. Assistance to participants in finding jobs, continuing their education, or entering additional training.
7. Collecting and analyzing information on postprogram outcomes.
8. Linking youth development activities under this Act with employer and industry strategies for upgrading workers' skills.

Integrating academic and occupational learning is not the responsibility of educators alone. School-to-work requires a partnership among elementary, secondary, and postsecondary educational institutions; private and public employers; community-based organizations; labor organizations; parents; students; state and local education agencies; and training and human service agencies. Collaboration among these groups is needed to link education reform with economic growth and workforce development in the United States.

Postsecondary Institutions

Career centers that focus on the needs of students in postsecondary institutions should provide programs or offer experiences that address a broad range of issues. It is sometimes the case that the bulk of student career development prior to postsecondary enrollment focused on getting into college or a training program and often did not consider what they might do once there (which highlights the problem of students making decisions in high school for which they are not developmentally prepared). This situation is sometimes further complicated by college career centers that primarily focus on helping students make the next transition from the postsecondary institution to work (e.g., they primarily focus on placement rather than the much broader career development process). Often, career development in postsecondary institutions falls on the shoulders of advisors.

The National Academic Advising Association (NACADA) addressed the importance of career development and planning when discussing standards and guidelines for academic advising programs in postsecondary institutions by utilizing the Academic Advising Standards and Guidelines created by the Council for the Advancement of Standards (CAS) for Student Services/ Development Programs. (You can reach NACADA at: NACADA Executive Office, Kansas State University, 2323 Anderson Avenue, Suite 225, Manhattan, KS 66502, Phone: 785-532-5717, FAX: 785-532-7732, email: nacada@ksu.edu, Web: http://www.ksu.edu/ nacada).

These standards stated that "the primary purpose of the academic advising program is to assist students in the development of meaningful educational plans that are compatible with their life goals." Further, they added that "the ultimate responsibility for making decisions about educational plans and life goals rests with the individual student. The academic advisor should assist by helping to identify and assess alternatives and the consequences of decisions."

In terms of student needs, many postsecondary students require assistance from staff involved in career development in these four areas (adapted from Herr and Cramer 1996):

1. The selection of a major field of study
2. Self-assessment and self-analysis
3. Understanding the world of work
4. Making decisions

It is important for postsecondary career centers to recognize and reinforce the broader career development process when working with students rather than focusing on the outcome (finding a job) alone. This focus on the process of career development prepares students to meet their immediate goals as well as increasing their chances of meeting their long-term goals.

Colleges and universities have used five major approaches to meet the career development needs of students: "(1) courses, workshops, and seminars that offer structured group experiences in career planning; (2) group counseling activities that are generally less structured and emphasize broader, more affective aspects of human and career development; (3) individual counseling opportunities that accentuate diverse theoretical orientations to career concerns; (4) placement programs that culminate the career planning and decision-making process; and (5) computerized placement services" (Herr and Cramer 1996).

Summary

Within an educational setting, career centers should educate students and faculty about their services and promote the expansion of career-related activities into the curricula. The centers should seek to contribute to the students' career development by

- teaching students the skills necessary to answer the three primary questions (*Who am I?*, *Where am I going?*, and *How do I get there?*) when they are developmentally ready to learn and use them,
- helping faculty connect course material to the world of work, and

- strengthening critical career development competency areas by having students apply their knowledge and skills to increasingly complex situations.

These generalized pursuits have specific manifestations at the different educational levels:

Elementary

Career centers might focus on identifying interests and aptitudes, connecting skills with occupations, connecting school with the world of work, and showing how to use information for planning.

Middle School or Junior High

Career centers might focus on how personal qualities and attributes relate to one's career, future educational and training opportunities and how to qualify for them, the broad range of career choices available and how to obtain information about them.

Secondary

Career centers might focus on developing and implementing individual career plans, the introduction of placement into career guidance, and the advantages and disadvantages of all the postsecondary options open to students.

Postsecondary

Career centers might focus on selecting a major field of study, self-assessment and self-analysis, understanding and experiencing the world of work, and placement programs and services.

Chapter 7

Serving Diverse Student Populations

by Judith Ettinger

As one walks through the halls of a high school or middle school that has a career center, one can recognize a successful career center. It is busy. Students are involved in the center in groups or individually. Staff use the center resources and send their students to the career center to complete a variety of assignments. There are luncheons scheduled in the career center on topics such as ways to meet with employers, resume writing, financial aid, and resources on the Internet. In the evenings, there are formal meetings with parents and students or students work on computers.

And then there are career centers that are not as successful. They are empty, silent, not easily accessible, and have little connection to the school curriculum. The space is used for activities that are not career-related. They do not have a defined role in the school.

How do the successful ones become one of the hubs of the school? Part of the success is due to location and physical appearance. The career center is in the mainstream of user traffic. The space is easily accessible by all students. There is sufficient room to accommodate small groups. There are quiet areas. There is a relaxed and casual, yet serious atmosphere in the career center. The staff have created and support a user-friendly, nonthreatening environment by adopting the philosophy that each enrolled student deserves full access to information and opportunities and that the career development process should be part of each student's preparation for his or her life in the workforce and in the community.

But philosophy is not enough to guarantee success. Staff must implement their philosophy by defining and working toward concrete goals. For example, career centers that focus on student needs have goals such as

- providing accurate and relevant career materials to all students;
- assisting in the research of students' and faculty's occupational ideas;
- offering career assessment to help students develop awareness of their interests, values and abilities; and
- providing career-related instruction to students and faculty.

Aside from the students themselves, another very important audience for the career center is the school's faculty members. For a career center to link successfully to students, faculty need to be engaged in the workings of the center. They need to incorporate the resources of the center into their curriculum and assignments, understanding the importance of the career center so that they use it to augment their lesson plans. For example, a number of schools require that each student complete a career portfolio. At New Brunswick High School in New Jersey, all students must complete a portfolio as part of their high school education. Career development portfolios are housed in the career center. Students work on their portfolios in classes and in the career center. They use the career center in every grade as part of a structured, formal program to complete a section of their portfolios. Not only are the portfolios stored in the career center, but all work completed by the students while they are engaged in the career development curriculum is kept in the career center. It is part of every student's curriculum and all faculty members are involved in implementing it.

Needs Assessment

The services offered by a career center are identified by the completion of a needs assessment, which is discussed in greater detail in Chapter Two. The needs assessment also helps to identify the best approach to use. It identifies the needs of specific groups such as non-college-bound students, girls and women, or those who are heading down divergent paths. The needs assessment should be done with five groups: administration, support staff, faculty, students, and parents. Examples of what might be highlighted in the results of a needs assessment include

- providing accurate and relevant career materials;
- assisting the students in researching occupational ideas suited to their interests, values and abilities;
- offering career assessment through testing and interest inventories;
- providing the faculty with staff and resources to support career related instruction; and
- providing an avenue for parents to participate in students career goals.

(Guthrie, Maxwell, Mosier, Nadaskay, and Vallejos 1990)

Strategies and Techniques

Given these needs, what day-to-day operations, strategies, and techniques can schools use to connect students with the career center? To reach all students, career centers should consider three approaches to delivering services (Schutt 1996):

1. Individual—such as completing assessment instruments, engaging in computer-assisted work, watching videotapes and meeting individually with a center staff member;
2. Small groups—such as job seeking or career exploration groups, math anxiety workshops, or work groups that identify accommodations for those with disabilities; and
3. Large groups—where issues such as financial assistance can be discussed with students and parents or visits by local employers can be scheduled.

The kinds of services that connect students to career centers include the following activities:

- Alumni mentoring
- Brown-bag lunches focusing on career development topics
- Career counseling
- Career days
- Community advisory group meetings

- Community referrals
- Co-op and internship experiences
- Corporate testing services
- Employment advising
- Freshman orientation activities
- General assessment of students and staff
- Inservice activities on career development for staff
- Job fairs
- Job readiness skills, such as preparing for interviews
- On-campus recruiting
- Outplacement counseling
- Panel discussions with experts
- Research and evaluation
- Resource files and databases
- Resume writing
- Self-development activities to raise awareness of skills and interests
- Study skills in small groups
- Volunteer employment opportunities

It is therefore critical to continually evaluate the perceived student benefit. An analysis of services should encompass a review of three areas:

- Access
- Comprehensive and coordinated services delivered at the career center
- Student benefits

The following examples illustrate the different approaches by career centers to take these goals and connect them effectively with their students.

Chesapeake College in Maryland links to students in several ways. Center staff go to the K-12 schools and meet with students and staff to provide numerous services in their career centers. These include career counseling individually and in groups, assistance in job readiness skills, administration of career interest tests, job placement services, resume writing workshops, job search strategies, and interviewing techniques. They also organize the annual career and job expo for area high schools, college students, and the community. In this way, they bring students onto campus and into the career center. Although they are very successful in providing services both to students enrolled in the college and to the larger community, they are still challenged by the need to find better ways to market their services to students and the community. Their successes are based on their belief in the importance of career planning to each student's education and life planning.

The Massachusetts Center for Career and Technical Education uses a different route to meeting the career development needs of students. They reach out to students through their teachers, administrators, and counselors. This career center was established as a professional development resource center for educators. At the center the staff delivers technical assistance to public schools and postsecondary institutions throughout Massachusetts. They also maintain computers at the center that can track databases, maintain mailing lists, and search for resources. The center library contains 5,000 items in print, video, and on CD and laser disks.

At the Mount Wachusett Community College in Gardner, Massachusetts, staff operate according to the philosophy that each enrolled student is entitled to full access to career information and career opportunities. Staff work to make the career development process part of each student's preparation for professional life and part of the commitment each student makes during his or her education. Staff encourage each student as an individual with unique academic and career goals. They work with a diversity of students including individuals with disabilities, returning adult students, single parents, part-time students, ESL students, and at-risk youth.

The career centers in Wisconsin were established to provide comprehensive career education planning and job training information, including information on options after high school in vocational and technical programs, four-year college degrees, youth apprenticeships and other work experiences related to the youth's education. Each career center was planned and established by local partnerships, including a combination of public and private school districts, universities and technical colleges, business and industry, community organizations, and other local partners. Each career center used a unique approach to connect youth and staff. For example, the Community Career Counseling Center system for Dane County in Wisconsin is a decentralized network of career counseling sites in schools, job service offices, the technical college, public libraries and community organizations. The career center in Green Bay, Wisconsin, is a large centralized career center staffed with career specialists and equipped with career computer software, videos, and written materials. Another mode of linking with students is through a mobile unit, such as the one in western Wisconsin that makes customized school visits that provide access to computers, career software, and print and video materials.

Based on the experiences of these schools, considerations that can improve linkage between students and the career center include

- hours of operation offer a variety of options including evening hours, Saturday hours, and early morning hours;
- distribution of career center maps to all potential users;
- location in the mainstream of the building/campus or near public transportation;
- physically appealing environment that has comfortable furniture, a minimum of noise, windows, good lighting, and attractive and colorful wall decorations;
- open access to resources not dependent on the presence of staff;
- user-friendly files;
- interactive materials;
- access that meets the requirements of the Americans with Disabilities Act;
- materials covering a wide range of reading levels;
- policies that allow students and staff to check out materials; and
- a diverse staff.

Students with Specific Concerns

There are some groups of students who will need more specific responses to their career development needs. The following examples illustrate how a career center can ensure access for three of these groups—young women, students with disabilities, and members of minority ethnic groups.

Example 1: Girls and Women

To promote equity, the career center serves girls and women during all phases of career planning and specifically encourages them to open up their options and plan careers in fields which are traditionally male-dominated, such as science and high technology. To do this, activities are scheduled in the career center, such as bringing women scientists to speak at a brown bag luncheon. Materials that test one's knowledge and help students explore and define attitudes and ideas are highlighted. Activities to learn more about career planning and other issues in science, math, and high technology areas are also included along with

- Specific sections on careers in science and technology that provide an opportunity to explore questions such as: Why might you be interested in science and technology? What are some jobs in science and engineering? What life skills are required in the sciences?
- Articles, materials, videos, and computer-based career planning programs that combat stereotypes based on myths—especially those that frequently discourage females from entering careers in math, science, and high technology—and that highlight specific careers in the physical sciences, life sciences, earth sciences, engineering, and computer technology
- Information and work groups that confront math anxiety and provide activities and tips for those who are intimidated by, or having trouble in, mathematics
- Opportunities to explore specific careers through job shadowing and interviewing experiences or completion of a career search

- Bibliographies and materials that include examples of women in a wide variety of careers such as profiles of women at NASA
- Materials to help teachers, parents, and career development facilitators work more equitably with young women, e.g., tools to evaluate gender fairness in a classroom
- Resources such as print materials, videos, Internet sites, and information about organizations to learn more about science, technology, mathematics, and careers, including:

African American Women of Hope. Available from Bread and Roses Cultural Project, Inc., 330 West 42nd Street, New York, NY 10036

No More Frogs to Kiss: 99 Ways to Give Economic Power to Girls. Joline Godfrey. New York: HarperCollins, 1995.

Exploring Work: Fun Activities for Girls. WEEA Equity Resource Center, Education Development Center, Inc., 1996. Available from the Women's Educational Equity Act Resource Center

The Scientist Within You: Women Scientists from Seven Continents—Biographies and Activities. Rebecca Lowe Warren and Mary H. Thompsan. ACI Publishing, 1995.

Created Equal: The Lives and Ideas of Black American Innovators. J. M. Brodie. New York: W. Morrow, 1993.

There's No Such Thing as Women's Work (videotape). Women's Bureau of the U.S. Department of Labor

The Cornell Theory Center Math and Science Gateway http://www.tc.cornell.edu/Edu/MathSciGateway/

The Ada Project (TAP) Junior: http://www.cs.yale.edu/homes/tap/tap-junior.html

Expect the Best from Girls: http://www.academic.org/

Women in Technology International: http://www.witi.com/

Example 2: Students with Disabilities

The policies and practices of the career center need to ensure access for students with disabilities and full compliance with the Americans with Disabilities Act (ADA). Morally and ethically, the career center staff must adopt policies and practices that treat all individuals with respect. Laws also make it our legal responsibility to respect the civil rights of individuals with disabilities.

Both the content and delivery of career center resources need to be examined in this context. For example, computer-based career information delivery systems are an important resource in most career centers. Yet, most are not currently accessible to those with disabilities, whether they be visual, hearing, or physical disabilities. They rarely include information specific to the needs of individuals with disabilities. To meet the equity requirements for students with disabilities, the computer-based systems should

- include information on legal rights under the Americans with Disabilities Act (ADA), Section 504, and IDEA;
- inform the user of accommodations and available modifications;
- expose the user to role models who have a disability, thus opening options, broadening horizons, and increasing knowledge about accommodations, job tasks, work environments;
- enable users to proceed at their own pace;
- use graphics and video to motivate;
- provide opportunities to practice decision making, problem solving, and time management skills; and
- include modifications to the system that could include closed-caption computer digitized videos, visual alternatives to sounds, alternatives to keyboard and mouse use, audio version of text or graphics.

Earlier in the chapter, the career center environment was referred to as one that needs to be nonthreatening and user friendly. What does that mean when we are talking about meeting the specific needs of individuals with disabilities? It means that staff need to be familiar enough with the ADA to help students redefine their disability status into areas of functional limitations that will affect job performance. They then need to help students identify accommodations that could be used to successfully function at that job. It means that there need to be, for example, parking spaces that are close to the center, modification of equipment, available qualified readers or sign language interpreters, higher desks and tables for wheelchair access, open aisles to allow wheelchairs into all areas of the center, and policies that allow students to remove materials from the center.

In terms of serving students with disabilities more effectively, career center staff members need to

- establish creative partnerships with special education faculty members to develop the most effective programs possible;
- understand the ADA and concepts such as job analysis and reasonable accommodations to teach students how to protect their civil rights;
- be advocates for all students with employers, students, co-workers, employees;
- know about resources in the community and maintain an informational folder; and
- not only assure accessibility but also actively communicate with all students about which materials can be prepared in alternative formats on request and by offering assistance procuring materials and serving as scribes or readers.

Example 3: Diverse Ethnic Groups

Diversity requires additional attention so that all youth and adults will receive the full benefits of the career center. Addressing the career-related needs of specific ethnic groups can be enhanced with knowledge of different cultural values and their relationship to work values. Differences in ethnic and social roots create a need for career center staff to understand identity issues, the value of appropriate role models, and the need for motivational strategies to set high expectations. Traditional stereotypes of occupational status and roles need to be addressed and challenged to help students expand their career options. The goal, as with all other students, is to prepare students to make informed decisions about career opportunities.

How does one build a supportive environment in the career center that works for all students and at the same time is sensitive to the career development needs of diverse ethnic groups? The career center needs to foster a sense of belonging. This can be done through respect for individuals and their culture and values and concomitant respect that can be shown through selection of materials that are congruent with their culture and values. For Latino students this might involve having resources in different languages (English and Spanish) and resources that recognize the difficulties inherent in the potential clash that could occur between Latino and Anglo cultures.

As with all students, preconceived ideas about what students are suited for are inappropriate. Instead, staff should provide students and adults with opportunities to identify personal interests, work-based learning experiences and opportunities to explore careers of interest, and resources so that students can discover their abilities. In addition, parents and other family members can be included in career center activities as frequently as possible to show personal and genuine concern for students and their significant others.

The Hispanic Dropout Project (1998) suggests five areas of focus that make a difference in a student's education. They have implications for activities in the career center:

- Stress high academic and behavior goals.
- Find ways to clearly communicate high expectations and standards.
- Create a climate in which interactions are respectful and supportive.
- Provide opportunities to find relevancy in academic activities.
- Integrate families in understanding the importance of working closely with their children to develop and monitor career plans so that informed career decisions can be made.

Summary

Linking to students begins with the development of a philosophy and goals that focus on the career development needs of all students. This philosophy and the accompanying goals need to form a blueprint for all activity in the career center. It is this frame of reference that moves the activities and events in the career center from a "cookbook" approach to education to a process that improves the career development of all students. In attempting to serve diverse student populations, school districts can improve their chances at success by

- continually revisiting the needs of the students, faculty, and community to be sure that the activities in the career center change with the needs of the school;
- ensuring that the career center does not become a space that is used for a wide variety of school-related activities but instead is reserved for career-related programs;
- keeping an eye on students who have special career development needs and ensuring that there is always a place for them in the career center; and
- keeping faculty, parents, and the community involved and informed of the career center's activities and successes.

Chapter 8

Adult Career Centers: An Overview

by April Schnell and Kathleen Schaefers,
with Barb Taylor and Eric Schnells

The work world has changed drastically in the last 20 years, with major shifts in how work, jobs, and careers are structured. Instead of traditional hierarchical structures and defined jobs, work is increasingly organized around projects and temporary contracts, with an emphasis on flexibility. Adults and organizations are rethinking and recreating their roles in this changing world of work. If visionaries such as William Bridges (1994) and Douglas T. Hall (1996) are right, these trends will not only continue but increase in scope into the next millennium.

Changes in the world of work have had a profound impact on the need for career services for adults. In addition to field-specific expertise, today's workers need sophisticated career management skills. Career centers can help adults develop the myriad of skills needed to survive and even thrive in this turbulent work environment.

To meet these needs, career centers are cropping up in a variety of settings and offering a plethora of services. Common sites include state workforce centers (serving all employee groups including managers), career centers at major corporations, outplacement firms, nonprofit community-based career centers, continuing education career centers, virtual career careers, and college career offices (which increasingly service alumni).

Not all career services, however, are provided at career centers having a physical location. Virtual career services, and other centers that deliver services at client locations, are becoming more common. Throughout this chapter the term *career centers* will refer to the wide variety of adult career centers and services available.

This chapter outlines the necessary steps in setting up a career center to serve adults. We will clarify what *adult* means, highlight key services and resources to reach this population, and give some examples of successful centers. We will also describe important considerations in career center service evaluation.

Characteristics of the Adult Population

Adult career centers have the challenge of meeting the career development needs of an extremely diverse population. To say *adult* usually indicates client age that ranges from 18 to retirement and beyond. This broad client definition means that diverse gender, ethnic identification, ability, orientation, and socio-economic backgrounds are included in adult populations.

Adults seek services for diverse reasons. Events such as layoffs or organizational restructuring precipitate the need for assistance. Technological advances and the subsequent changes in work tasks and flow often result in the need for retooling and occupational or job transitions. Flattened organizational structures and fewer promotional opportunities (and hence more plateaued workers) contribute to the need for career enrichment plans. Life events such as changes in the family (e.g., divorce, the addition of children) or life stage (e.g., retirement) also create a need for career assistance.

Adults are increasingly using career centers for more personal reasons as well. With all the turbulence in the workplace, more and more adults are rethinking the role of work in their lives. Adults are frequently looking for work that goes beyond the utilization of their skills. They are exploring jobs that are fulfilling in a personal way and which fit with their interests, values, personality, and sometimes life mission.

In addition, career professionals are seeing clients who want to realign their life commitments to achieve balance. As the twenty-first century approaches, we are witnessing a trend toward lifestyle simplification (Celente 1997). Many adults are reevaluating lifestyle choices and finding ways to simplify their lives to be more in balance with their values and life priorities. Saltzman

(1991) used the term *downshifter* to describe adults who modify work commitments to allow time for other areas of their lives, reflecting personal values and life fulfillment. According to Kennedy (1997), human resource professionals are reporting that for workers under 35, "time has replaced money as the most desired perk." Career professionals are assisting clients in their efforts to achieve greater life/work balance by helping them identify life-role priorities, evaluate options, and refashion their work (Hansen 1997).

Given the diversity in the adult population and their issues, career centers must be versatile and adaptable. Career professionals must continually update their skills and knowledge to keep pace with the changing needs of the adult population. Career centers must devise creative and cost-effective approaches to reach their clientele. For their centers to grow or just to survive, many career professionals will have to gain skills in areas such as marketing, grant-writing, and generating revenue.

Developmental Issues of Adults

Despite the diversity of adult clientele, there are some developmental considerations common to adults that can serve as guides. The National Occupational Information Coordinating Committee (1989) has created Career Development Competencies and Indicators for Adults. They are designed to strengthen and improve career development centers, and are organized around three major career developmental areas: (1) Self-Knowledge, (2) Educational and Occupational Exploration, and (3) Career Planning.

Self-knowledge evolves in many ways, through the medley of life experiences and through introspection. Personal and career-related experiences shape one's understanding of the world of work and help define one's views of self in relation to work. Experiences often shape our self-image, even our identities (i.e., "I am a leader" or "I am a carpenter").

Self-knowledge has long been a cornerstone of traditional career development thinking. Career professionals routinely help adults

111

assess their interests, skills, values, expectations, and personality, and relate this self-understanding to the world of work.

Such self-knowledge becomes even more important in adapting to a changing workplace. To respond to change, adults must have a clear understanding of their assets and abilities, and know how to market themselves. Clients must continually identify skills deficits, as well as knowledge and skills they want to learn, so that they can develop learning plans throughout their lives. They must be adaptable to shifting market currents.

Adults often hold preconceived expectations about work that do not fit with the rapidly changing world of work. For example, many adults hold a strong belief that once they complete their traditional education, they should be "finished" or "done" with career development. With adult populations, the career professional may initially spend time describing career development as a normal lifelong process. Once this foundation has been laid, many adults then identify their need for a sense of control and desire to be proactive (versus reactive) in their career development. Adults who have allowed others to define their career choices (employers, parents, spouse) often embark on a journey of discovering their own personal interests, values and skills, and nurturing a sense of autonomy. Individual career desires can then be held up to, or matched with, opportunities within the world of work (Bridges 1994).

In the area of *educational and occupational exploration,* the primary need of many adults is to understand the new and dynamic world of work. Although most adults have seen changes in the world of work from their positions in the workforce, they often lack the language to describe the changes they have seen. In addition, they may also lack a larger perspective of those changes in the whole idea of work, beyond the perhaps small slice they have experienced firsthand. The dynamic world of work requires that individuals possess career self-reliance, or the attitude of being self-employed whether inside or outside of an organization (Collard, Waterman, and Waterman 1994). The concept of career self-reliance is new for most adults, and can be both challenging and refreshing. The ability to understand the ongoing changes then requires specific skills such as being able to use labor market information and maintaining contacts with professionals in fields of interest to determine what's out there.

For adults considering a career change, there is a strong need to identify which skills are marketable in order to stay competitive as a job applicant, as well as to assist in finding training opportunities for lifelong learning. Just as organizations engage in the process of benchmarking, comparing internal work processes to those of the competition with the goals of identifying and implementing best practices, so also do adults find it helpful to compare their skill sets with those of other workers in their occupation. Adults seeking career or job changes may then also need coaching on the skills of networking, positioning and marketing themselves for a new occupation.

Many adults are not looking for a career change, but rather to find a fit with a current position, or current organization. In these situations, common needs of adult employees include

- seeing clearly how one's position contributes to the success of the organization,
- having the knowledge base to be a successful employee,
- having access to training opportunities, and
- receiving periodic feedback which is helpful in improving performance.

Finally, in the area of *career planning,* many adults need to broaden their perspectives, to see multiple options. They need to sharpen their skills to overcome barriers, evaluate options, make decisions, and manage transitions. Career professionals need to adopt a holistic approach to career planning with adults. They assist clients in everything from learning to manage stress to cultivating support to understanding life roles and improving work/life balance.

Identifying the common developmental issues of adult clientele, using the framework of self-knowledge, educational and occupational exploration, and career planning, is a solid foundation upon which to begin the steps of building a successful adult career center.

Steps in Setting Up an Adult Career Center

When examining existing career centers or exploring the possibility of setting one up , there are six major considerations:

1. Who will create the adult career center?
2. Is your client the individual, the organization, or both?
3. Who is the population to be served?
4. Where and how will center services be provided?
5. What are the funding sources of the career center?
6. Who will be the service providers for the adult career center?

As we explore the answers to these questions, we will also highlight the steps in establishing an adult career center (Wagner 1993):

Step 1: Select a coordinator
Step 2: Secure administrative support
Step 3: Select a steering committee
Step 4: Identify customers and clientele
Step 5: Prepare a written statement of purpose
Step 6: Determine client needs
Step 7: Decide how the center will meet those needs
Step 8: Prepare a statement of goals and objectives
Step 9: Determine the most effective delivery system
Step 10: Prepare a detailed plan
Step 11: Ensure coordination with existing centers
Step 12: Investigate funding sources
Step 13: Select staff
Step 14: Conduct orientation
Step 15: Identify, evaluate, and order materials

Who Will Create the Adult Career Center?

Step 1: Select a coordinator
Step 2: Secure administrative support
Step 3: Select a steering committee

When creating an adult career center, several models are feasible. The following questions should be considered to ascertain the appropriate model for a given organization or population. Will a task force, advisory board, consulting organization, or director and his or her staff create the center? Gutteridge, Leibowitz, and Shore (1993) found that almost half of organizational career center respondents effectively used a task force or advisory group to design or implement their centers. Are these creators career development experts, trained human resource professionals, members of the population to be served, other stakeholders, or some combination of the above? Are the creators on-staff, hired on a salary or contract basis, or volunteers? Will there be an ongoing steering committee?

An example of how one organization grappled with these questions is described here. The University of Minnesota is a large, land-grant institution with approximately 37,600 students, 2,950 faculty, and 14,500 staff on its Twin Cities campuses. The university has a history of employee representation, including an active civil service employee group, faculty senate, and bargaining unit representation for its clerical, technical, and trades employees.

Employee groups and management were increasingly concerned about the perceived lack of promotional career opportunities for staff at the university. In response, human resources conceptualized and funded a pilot career development program for staff. A master's level counseling psychologist with career development expertise was hired to explore program options and design and deliver certain pilot services. The pilot lasted for one year and was well received by staff.

After the pilot year, a task force was established with representation from management and labor to decide whether or not a career development program would continue on an ongoing basis, and if so, to determine essential components and establish buy-in from administration and employee groups. Because of the university's culture of staff involvement, it was important that the program grow out of a collaborative venture. Provisions for the establishment of the Employee Career Enrichment Program (ECEP) became part of collective bargaining agreements with the American Federation of State, County and Municipal Employees (AFSCME).

ECEP was created by a joint labor/management task force, and they relied heavily on the guidance of career development professionals, human resource practitioners, and employee assistance counselors. Given the size and complexity of the University of Minnesota staff and culture, it was decided to position ECEP within the Office of Human Resources, and hire an in-house staff of career development professionals to provide services.

ECEP solicits ongoing feedback and guidance from an advisory board. The board provides input but does not control ECEP. Advisory board members include

- staff representatives, including civil service, bargaining unit, professional and administrative staff, and multicultural employee groups;
- faculty experts in the field of career development;
- human resources professionals; and
- training and development experts.

Is Your Client the Individual, the Organization, or Both?

Step 4: Identify customers and clientele
Step 5: Prepare a written statement of purpose

Career centers that cater to individuals (e.g., alumni) tailor services to the specific population segment that they serve. The needs and best interests of their identified population and individual clients define the center's priorities.

However, career centers may have the dual task of serving individuals within an organization and also the organization itself. For example, an organization may staff its own internal career center, providing services to employees and advancing organizational goals simultaneously. Alternatively, an organization may contract with a consulting firm to provide these services, again expecting some form of benefits for the organization.

Any time that a career professional has more than one client constituency, the objectives and roles of each constituency must be carefully assessed for compatibility. For example, a career center

116

may be charged by the parent organization with improving retention of employees. This goal may not be compatible with an individual employee's goal to find a more satisfying occupation outside the organization. While the organizational career development professional intends to consciously link people's career plans with the organization's workforce needs (Gutteridge, et al. 1993), the provider must attempt to find a balance between what may be conflicting agendas.

An example of an organizational career program that has succeeded as an in-house provider is Career Development and Transition Services (CDTS) at Allina Health. CDTS has been successful because their role is clearly defined as providing services to the employee client, thus supporting the organization.

Clear role definitions can assist with such organizational issues as redeployment of employees, problems that employees experience within the work environment, and individual employee goals to find new employment opportunities. In the case of a layoff or RIF, CDTS's role is to build employees' self-reliance so that they would know how to find a new position within the organization. For work environment problems, CDTS helps employees to better articulate their issues. Staff then make appropriate referrals, when necessary, to other human resource groups like the employee assistance program, organization development, employee relations for nonrepresented groups, and employee health. In some cases, feedback about observed trends may be given to human resources without compromising individual employee confidentiality. Finally, Allina Health System supports employees' career development goals, even if it occasionally means the employee eventually leaves the organization. Follow-up data shows, however, that CDTS is actually a retention tool, since approximately 75 percent of employees who receive services during the first three years remain employed within the organization. If an employee does choose to leave the organization, Allina receives the benefit of the goodwill of that person for the assistance and services they received from Career Development and Transition Services.

To clearly identify the role of career services within an organization, it is important to understand the sponsoring organization's motivation for providing career services to employees. Gutteridge, Leibowitz, and Shore (1993) surveyed a large number of American institutions (corporate and government) to learn more about their motivations for providing career development services to their employees. In the corporate sample, the top two responses were "a desire to develop or promote from within" and "a shortage of promotable talent." Government respondents indicated that "organizational commitment" and "employee interest" were the top motivations for having career development centers. For both groups, other responses included "desire to motivate employees under conditions of limited organizational growth" and "development of organization's strategic plan." Having a clear understanding of organizational drivers at the start can have a great impact on the services provided and the methods of assessment used.

Who Is the Population to Be Served?

> Step 6: Determine client needs
> Step 7: Decide how the center will meet those needs
> Step 8: Prepare a statement of goals and objectives

In setting up a new center, valuable questions to ask may include the following: Will services be limited to those within an organization? Will services be limited to certain segments of an organization? Will services be offered to supervisors as well as employees? Will services be offered to a community at large? Will the cost of the services preclude certain populations from accessing services? How, and to whom, will services be marketed? Will the services be limited by the expertise of the staff? Will availability of other resources (e.g., time, money) limit the services? Will the population served be limited by the times and places services are offered? To some degree, the scope of services, how they are provided, and how they are marketed will limit the population served.

Student Services, part of University College at the University of Minnesota, has found a very inclusive way to identify their client population: "prospective and current adult evening students." Student Services provides services to the metropolitan community at large, including a range of economic, ethnic, and age diversity. This necessitates that the counselors be skilled at working effectively with a wide variety of people juggling life roles.

Career development counseling (both individual and group) is just one part of the comprehensive services that these master's degree-level counselors provide to their clientele. Because helping clients answer the question "What do I want to do for a career?" can often mean the clients will return to school, counselors also provide academic advising services for all of the programs at the university. Many clients are then faced with questions of "How will I pay for my classes?", and so the counselors must also be well versed in financial aid advising. This triad of client services (career development plus academic and financial aid counseling) requires an extremely experienced and proficient staff, with long learning curves for new hires.

In addition, the structure of services offered, including time, place and cost, is designed to accommodate part-time adult learners, who represent the majority of students in University College. Appointments are offered days and evenings, Monday through Friday. While academic and financial aid advising are free, costs for career development counseling are offered at half the market rate. There is no extra charge for assessments. Counseling services are primarily offered at the campus location. In addition, academic and financial aid advising is provided by the career development staff at inner city locations.

Services are marketed in four ways. First, University College regularly puts out a comprehensive Evening Class Bulletin, distributed to locations around the Twin Cities. Second, the services are internally marketed to other college advisors of related programs. Next, University College's own degree programs are offered collaboratively with local community colleges, and marketed at these locations as well. Finally, information and orientation groups are offered around the community several times monthly.

With the combination of this comprehensive marketing plan, highly skilled counselors, and services that are extremely user friendly, *prospective* students receive career development guidance and often become *current* students. Student Services at

University College is successful in their goal to provide services for adult learners.

Where and How Will Center Services Be Provided?

Step 9:   Determine the most effective delivery system
Step 10: Prepare a detailed plan
Step 11: Ensure coordination with existing centers

Will there be a physical career center? If so, what kind of space is needed? Will there be offices, confidential counseling space, a resource room, or meeting facilities? How will the center be organized? Will there be stations or areas where materials with a common focus are grouped for clients (Wagner 1993)? In what location will the facility be? Is parking available for staff and clients? Is the location conveniently accessible for clients of all abilities? Does the location convey the appropriate marketing impression to potential clients? What physical equipment and furnishings are really necessary and which are simply desirable? And finally, if an information resource area is planned, will there be a balance of print, nonprint, and computer-assisted materials?

When American Express Financial Advisors decided to offer career development services to employees, the director held focus groups to let the employees decide what kind of a site they wanted. The employees strongly insisted that there be a physical center. A physical space is what the term *career center* meant to them. They wanted their center to have books, videos, worktables and counselor office space. The employees also felt that private spaces for clients would be a good idea. Based on this input, the computer terminals (where employees can do career exploration, resume writing, job searching) are located in walled off areas, tucked away from the main traffic flow in the center. The finished center is approximately 1,000 square feet, including a private conference room.

Part of the center, which holds the computer terminals and handouts, is accessible 24 hours a day, seven days a week. The library resource collection is only open during business hours. The center feels very "homey," which encourages drop-in visits. Employees can access any service as a walk-in with the exception of one-on-one counseling, which requires an appointment. The budget for materials is adequate to keep resources current.

The center is housed in the home office location, the IDS tower in downtown Minneapolis. While American Express has several business locations, the majority of employees work at the home office. Housing the center at the home office was intentional. The location sends the message that the career development program is an integral part of American Express.

American Express employees were also involved in giving the career center its identity. A contest was held among employees to arrive at the name of Career Enrichment Center (CEC). In addition, an employee design team created a logo identity for the center that not only appears on CEC materials, but also on signs directing clients to the correct floor and location of the center within the building. A large banner with this logo hangs on the wall of the center, welcoming clients.

The library resource collection includes a good balance of print and nonprint materials. There are two dedicated personal computers which contain the Discover program, internal job postings (both for local and international locations), and Wilson Learning Corporation's Creating Your Dream. Other career software tutorials include topics like resume writing and mentoring. Educational audio and videotapes are also available.

What are the alternatives if a physical center is not suitable, possible, or adequate? In this age of just-in-time, highly customized services for a global workforce, career service providers must creatively meet the time, place, and resource needs of their clients. Physical resources can be expensive and quickly outdated. Virtual career centers have become cutting edge, offering information and more, 24 hours a day, wherever potential clients have computers and Internet accesses. The Talent Alliance is entirely a virtual career development center discussed later in this chapter. (See also Chapter Eleven.)

American Express's Career Enrichment Center has Internet features to supplement its physical center. For example, a virtual bulletin board provides information about services and allows employees to sign up for counseling and workshops online. The CEC is also investigating the possibility of creating an intranet. At this time, CEC computer terminals do not have access to the World Wide Web. However, clients are sometimes introduced to the Web during individual counseling sessions.

What Will Be the Funding Sources of the Career Center?

Step 12: Investigate funding sources

How do the bills get paid? Most adult career centers have a clear sense of whether they are nonprofit, for-profit, or reporting to an organization which is nonprofit or for-profit. Depending on the funding source, the mission may change. For-profit career centers will also need to focus some resources on generating business, or demonstrating a return on investment. Nonprofit career centers may need to generate operating funds, perhaps by securing grant funds or identifying donations.

Who Will Be the Service Providers for the Career Center?

Step 13: Select staff
Step 14: Conduct orientation
Step 15: Identify, evaluate, and order materials

Will services be provided by professionals who have training, current employees to be trained, or members of the population to be served? Are the service providers paid or volunteer? What staff skill sets are desirable for center effectiveness? How will staff performance be evaluated? Currently, career professionals most commonly hail from the fields of counseling, organizational development, and human resources. The National Board for Certified Counselors (NBCC) offers two different professional certifications: the National Career Counselor Certification (NCCC) and the Certified Career Development Facilitator (CCDF) credential. The purpose of having specialty credentials is that they identify the educational background, knowledge, skills, and competencies of the specialist in career development.

Beyond specific career counseling and career development skills, Wagner (1993) recommended the inclusion of other desirable capacities or staff functions, such as managing a resource collection, job placement, curriculum development, and community resource development and coordination. Professionals at the University of Minnesota's Employee Career Enrichment Program have found the following skill sets to be useful:

- Understanding organizational career development issues
- Ability to work collaboratively with many constituent groups
- Ability to align the program with other human resource initiatives
- Responsiveness to changing organizational priorities
- Marketing and communication skills
- Program evaluation skills

Important Considerations for Adult Career Centers

Critical Services

Critical services for individual clients usually include some combination of counseling, assessment, consultation, seminars and workshops, and provision of placement and labor market information. Although these services may look like the same components of a successful adult career development center 20 years ago, much has changed. As the number of clients and their needs increases, and resources become ever tighter, career professionals have recognized the need for greater productivity and efficiency in delivering services. The balance in the combination of services used has often shifted. Where individual counseling may have been the primary delivery mode of services in the past, today's professional may focus more on group work. For example, the University of Minnesota's Employee Career Enrichment Program (ECEP) encourages employees to participate first in their workshop series, designed to address common needs of adults in a university work environment. Participants start with an orientation to career development, and progress through self-assessment and action-oriented workshops, customizing their enrollment choices to meet individual goals. Workshops are participatory, and utilize facilitated peer discussion exercises to personalize workshop content. Follow-up one-on-one consultations with trained career counselors are provided, allowing the counselor and client to efficiently build on what was learned through the workshops.

Critical Connections

To be successful, adult career centers need to establish a network of influence. Critical relationships can mean partnering with other external organizations, such as employers, state agencies, and other community service organizations. For organizational career centers, by definition part of larger systems, critical relationships can mean integration with human resources structures, procedures, policies, and groups, such as staffing professionals, organizational development consultants, training centers, Equal Employment Opportunity (EEO) functional groups, and unions. To form critical relationships, career professionals must devote energy to clearly communicating both the mission and the value added by the services provided. Career center evaluation results can be a very useful tool in communicating service effectiveness.

Challenges in Serving Adults

Time limitations and career choice restrictions are very real for adults. These limitations affect clients' abilities to seek and continue with services, as well as following up with action plans or homework. Family obligations and time limitations may also be factors in increased location restrictions for adults. Depending on the size of the city or town where the adults reside, they may have less flexibility in seeking services, making decisions, and acting on plans.

These limitations affect how career professionals structure and deliver services. For example, while adults can benefit from peer contact and support, traditional support groups are often difficult to set up due to scheduling conflicts and challenges in attending meetings at a set place and time. Brown bag, short term, and open membership groups can enable clients to get the group support they desire, while still maintaining some time commitment and location flexibility for clients. Alternatively, virtual support has the advantage of being accessible 24-hours a day, from any

Internet-accessible terminal. Some concerns for career counseling or coaching online include limitations of communication without visual cues and questionable electronic confidentiality (Sampson, Kolodinsky, and Greeno 1997).

Current work situations can also affect how and if adults use career centers. For example, does the client have organizational or supervisory support for career development? Is the client in a work role which is classified as exempt, salaried nonexempt, or hourly, and how does that classification relate to self-image and the availability of services and resources?

For a full discussion of the way adult career development concerns differ from those of young people, consult Chapter Nine, which also covers a new and promising way to meet those concerns.

Career Centers and the World Wide Web

The look and feel of career centers has changed dramatically in recent years. Resource libraries containing expensive volumes of information ranging from current to obsolete are being replaced by computer laboratories with Internet access to information that is up-to-date, prescreened, and organized for client convenience.

An example of a career center that uses the World Wide Web to reach clients is the University of Minnesota's Employee Career Enrichment Program (ECEP). The ECEP Web Site (URL http://www.umn.edu/ohr/ecep) is a compilation of resources created and assembled by the ECEP staff for university employees. In selecting links to sites created outside of the university, the ECEP staff uses a guiding principle of selectivity over inclusion. In other words, ECEP staff filters through the vast array of career-related resources on the Web and steers employees to those that are most useful and well presented. This decision was made to reduce the very real potential for information overload. It is important to note that because information available online is constantly changing, staff must continuously update the Web site.

In addition to Web pages, technologies such as online bulletin boards provide learning opportunities with others that share an interest in specific career areas. Chat rooms and email have opened the door to online career coaching, either individually or in a virtual group. Listservs, such as the National Association of Colleges and Employer's Jobplace, assist career professionals in keeping each other informed of new developments and information available within the field of career development.

Organizational Career Development Centers

Adult career centers within organizations face the additional challenge of providing information about the internal (within the organization) world of work structure. In addition to the usual individual client services, career centers for organizations might include development centers (training), internal labor market information, job matching systems, and organizational potential assessment processes. (Gutteridge, et al. 1993).

As career development professionals have increasingly used technology to enhance career services, many organizations have developed customized intranet career resources to provide these services in just-in-time fashion. Intranet, which is a network only available to those inside an organization, can provide services to employees or clients of that organization who may be located around the world. State-of-the-art resources have the ability to link results of performance appraisals, available training opportunities, self-assessments, and internal job postings that permit the user to automatically submit an application, all with the click of a mouse.

An example of an innovative intranet is the Talent Alliance (http://www.talentalliance.org). The Talent Alliance is a nonprofit coalition of organizations—business, industry, trade associations, professional services firms, government representatives, and educational institutions. Through their interactive intranet, member organizations and their employees have access to a plethora of career-related information and tutorials to help them make informed career and workplace decisions, including up-to-date research on work trends, business needs, workforce planning, career planning and development, and education and training.

For the individual employee, the Talent Alliance features a virtual Personal Growth Center. Through the network, users can progress through self-assessment exercises, research occupations, consult with an online career professional, develop an action plan, get recommendations for skill development, and even connect with people for informational interviewing.

For member organizations, the Talent Alliance features a Business Growth Center, which includes research, commentaries, benchmarks, and case studies pertinent to organizational managers and leaders. An applicant matching system is incorporated, pre-screening electronic resumes and portfolios from a talent pool and automatically alerting managers to appropriately skilled candidates.

This kind of intranet is innovative in its content and in its collaboration. The Talent Alliance provides a forum for member organizations to combine forces, benchmark practices, and share resources. The intranet, with its quick responsiveness and wide-reaching capabilities, makes this kind of organizational cooperation possible.

There is no doubt that technology is changing the face of career development. As the frontiers of technology applications in career counseling are explored, professionals are also faced with the need to discuss the ethical considerations (confidentiality, informed consent, etc.) which are necessary when using such technologies (Sampson, et al. 1997).

Career Center Evaluation

Center evaluation is critical to ensuring that career professionals meet the needs of the client constituencies served. Evaluation also provides direction for on-going center changes and improvements. There are at least four areas that career development centers attempt to evaluate: service quality, center usage, center effectiveness, and return on investment.

Quality of Services

Quality of services is most often translated into customer satis-faction. Many centers survey clients at the time of service deliv-ery, inquiring about the competency and expertise of providers, as well as the adequacy of resources and facilities. Survey results are easily and immediately obtained. However, a client's evaluation of quality will depend on that client's own expectations as well as the quality of the services.

Center Usage

Most career development centers are very effective at measuring center usage, that is, how much the center is used and by whom. Items measured may include a wide variety of clientele demo-graphics, as well as information on what combinations of services the clients use. Virtual career centers may simply record number of "hits" by page, or may request more detailed demographic information from the user.

Center Effectiveness

Evaluating human development centers can be challenging, par-ticularly in light of the prevailing value of measurable outcomes. Stakeholders and other center financiers ask for evidence of suc-cessful outcomes. Yet, when we talk about career development for a diverse population of adults, what is the desired outcome? There is no single answer that applies to all clients. And yet there are three key questions that we must consider. First, what has been the effect of the developmental activities? Next, is the client the best source of information when one is trying to determine if career development activities have been successful? Finally, when do we measure if the career development activity or intervention has been successful?

In measuring center effectiveness, the goal of "career self-reliance" (Collard 1994) lends itself well to evaluation measure-ment. Using this model, the measured outcome can be a new atti-tude, behavior, or acquired knowledge. Adult career centers can measure client self-knowledge, knowledge of the world of work, preparation and skills for participation in training and work, and the client's sense of empowerment and motivation for managing his or her own career. While most professionals agree that the individual client, the manager, and the organization share the responsibility for career development (Gutteridge, et al. 1994), individual "outcomes" are easiest to measure, particularly by centers that are not organizational centers. Finally, by measuring a client's new behaviors, as well as sense of empowerment and motivation, an immediate evaluation is possible. The assumption is made that the center has been successful in that it has given the client the information, skills, and motivation to act. Whether or not the client follows through on a personal action plan is often not measured.

Return on Investment

While center effectiveness is the way to determine "Is what we're doing working?", career development professionals are also asked to answer "Is it worth doing?" In the climate of justifying return on investment, do those who are paying the bills find the outcomes (even successful ones) worth the dollars spent? For centers servicing only individual clients, client satisfaction and referrals are the primary indicators that the dollars are well spent. For internal organization career centers, return on investment is difficult to measure. Many Fortune 500 corporate career development professionals are still looking for methods of measuring return on investment. Most organizations with career development centers possessed strong beliefs that in today's competitive business climate, human resource development is a necessary component of meeting organizational goals. External for-profit career centers in the outplacement industry continue to measure return on investment by quality of services as evidenced by time-to-placement and other client satisfaction measures.

Summary

There are six questions to consider when setting up an adult career center, corresponding to fifteen active steps to take toward answering those questions and reaching your goal.

Who will create the center?

Step 1: Select a coordinator
Step 2: Secure administrative support
Step 3: Select a steering committee
Is the client the individual, the organization, or both?
Step 4: Identify customers and clientele
Step 5: Prepare a written statement of purpose
Who is the population to be served?
Step 6: Determine client needs
Step 7: Decide how the center will meet those needs
Step 8: Prepare a statement of goals and objectives
When and how will services be provided?
Step 9: Determine the most effective delivery system
Step 10: Prepare a detailed plan
Step 11: Ensure coordination with existing centers
What are the funding sources?
Step 12: Investigate funding sources
Who will be the service providers?
Step 13: Select staff
Step 14: Conduct orientation
Step 15: Identify, evaluate, and order materials

Important Considerations for Adult Career Centers

- Critical Services
- Critical Connections
- Challenges of Serving Adults

Adult Career Center Evaluation

- Quality of Services
- Center Usage
- Center Effectiveness
- Return on Investment

Like young people, adults often have limited perceptions of the world of work and need to broaden their knowledge beyond their personal experiences. They have grown up with a limited knowledge of the processes used to effectively access and use career and labor market information. There are a number of differences, however. When one looks at the career development needs of adults, issues that single them out from their younger counter-

Chapter 9

Adult Career Centers: One-Stop Centers

by Judith Ettinger

parts are their past work experience, leisure time pursuits, family responsibilities, lack of geographic flexibility, and overall lifestyle. According to Zunker (1981), specific career issues of concern for adults who seek career development services include

- general lack of awareness of the wide range of occupations in the world of work;
- lack of direction;
- not having kept pace with changing job technologies, procedures, and practices;
- having only a single career orientation;
- lack of understanding of the benefits and problems that accompany a career change; and
- general feeling of unfulfillment in their present circumstances, and a search for challenge and meaning in their career.

Barriers faced by adults might include transportation, housing, family issues, language and literacy, coping with violence, legal issues, educational limitations, extreme financial difficulties, self-perceptions and self-esteem issues, day care, age, addiction, health problems, and fear of failure.

To meet these needs, a program must increase the knowledge base of an individual about self and the workplace while providing the support needed to overcome barriers. Hoppin (1994) believes that the focus of a career development initiative should lead to a better understanding of three components:

1. Self-knowledge, including:

Roles: identifying current and past roles in a way that helps clients look beyond past job titles to see how they have and will interact with the work environment;

Interests: looking at previous work and leisure activities and identifying what made these activities interesting or not interesting, with the focus on building a paying job out of those interests;

Values: a measure of the commitment the client brings to a particular job, helping to prioritize what role "work" plays among the client's many other roles;

Skills: awareness of skills gained from past work experiences and other experiences within family or the community;

Personal style: an understanding of personal style and how personality and work fit together;

Personal realities: financial obligations, budget, child care needs, age, available time to retrain, level of support from family and others, physical impairments that may affect career goals; and

Self-development needs: identifying areas that need work, such as increased skills levels, work habits, and personal image.

2. *Information on the workplace and the work environment,* referring to the accumulation of career-related information and identification of past and present experiences. When making a career-related decision, reflection upon that information becomes part of the decision making process. This also includes an analysis of the level of comfort in a work environment, i.e., are social needs being met? Is there a feeling of safety? Are there challenges?

3. *A system for obtaining and integrating information,* which can be derived from a number of models; for example, see Figure 3.

The last step is, effectively, the creation of an action plan. A goal is set and the necessary steps to reach that goal are documented. Goals vary in scope. They could be as specific as *Completing the one-day career assessment workshop at the career center* or as broad as *Developing a new career*. Regardless of the kind of goal, it is important to break the process of attainment into small, measurable steps. These steps should be placed on a timeline with an

Gather Information About:

Self . . .
Roles
Interests
Values
Skills and Aptitudes
Personal Style
Preferred Environments
Personal Realities
Developmental Needs

and

Work Responsibilities . . .
Research Occupations
Research Industries
Research the Labor Market

Make Decisions

Identify and
Evaluate Possibilities

Explore Alternatives

Choose an Option
(Short and Long-
term)

Develop An Action Plan

Set a Goal

Develop Steps Necessary to
Reach the Goal

Build in Support, Accountability,
and Rewards

Figure 3. (Adapted from Hoppin 1994)

**Career Development: Learning a Process—and a
Process of Learning**

133

indication of when completion should be achieved. Support and rewards should be build into the action plan.

Considering the amount of work that needs to be done to meet the career development needs of adults, it would appear that the need for services is broad and deep. Until recently, these needs were met through a fragmented and disjointed system of public and nonprofit agencies that dealt with career development issues piece by piece. Recently, the United States Department of Labor designed one-stop career centers to work with the multiple issues that adults bring to the career planning process.

One-Stop Career Centers

(http://www.ttrc.doleta.gov/onestop/)

The U.S. Department of Labor launched the one-stop career center initiative in 1994 in response to the perception that federal training and other employment-related service programs were fragmented, duplicative, and difficult to access by consumers and employers alike (Boetz 1997). The purpose of the centers was to create a continuum of services, including both federal and state training programs. Equal attention was paid to enhancing both public and employer access to services.

The one-stop centers were designed to meet the career development needs of adults. The centers "broker the labor exchange." They help career changers, students, college graduates, downsized employees, individuals moving from welfare to work, veterans, and workers with disabilities. When clients enter, they are greeted at the door and queried as to the type of assistance they need. If they are new to the center, they are typically given a short tour and shown to the resource room. Many clients only need this type of attention. Higher levels of service are available for those who might need to meet with a placement specialist, would like to join a group that teaches job search skills, or need information about unemployment benefits. The one-stop staff coordinates all the services needed including vocational rehabilitation, veterans support, postsecondary education, or unemployment compensation.

These centers have taken the simple idea of putting a number of related services under one roof with the goal of success for all workers. Under the one-stop roof, publicly funded employment and training services are brought together. Thus, the services are easier for both employers and job seekers to use. The centers blend programs, resources, and services, often including

- ADA regulations and vocational rehabilitation agencies
- Adult education
- Alcoholics Anonymous
- Child and adult day care services
- Church groups
- Community associations
- Community colleges
- Community mental health organizations
- County extension services
- County substance abuse programs
- Emergency housing
- Federal sources for rural resources
- Financial aid
- Hospital information phone lines
- Information about public transportation
- Legal aid
- Library services
- Parents without partners
- Private industry councils
- Salvation Army
- School counseling services
- Small Business Administration
- Spouse abuse center
- Suicide hotline
- Unemployment office
- United Way
- YWCA

The one-stop career centers make extensive use of computer-based information. There are four parts to the electronic structure. The U.S. Department of Labor's Employment and Training Administration has taken the lead in developing all four components. (The Web address for each component follows the short description.)

1. *America's Job Bank* contains posted job openings from local employment service offices. They are posted directly on the Internet. Each of the 50 states has its own accessible job bank that contributes to this one national job bank. (http://www.ajb.dni.us/)

2. *America's Talent Bank* contains electronic resumes that have been posted with local employment service offices and then posted on the Internet. Each state also has its own resume bank. Employers can search the bank to find candidates with the skills needed to fill their available positions. (http://www.atb.org/)

3. *American's Labor Market Information System* (ALMIS) delivers wage rates, occupational and industry projections, information about the labor supply, demand data, employment and unemployment statistics, employer profiles, area profiles, and occupational descriptions. (http://ecu-vax.cis.ecu.edu/~lmi/lmi.html)

4. *American's Training Network* is still in the design phase. When completed, it will contain both a national database of training opportunities and information on courses offered by traditional institutions and through distance learning.

In the future, there will be growing links between these four databases. For example, in the future, when one posts a resume it will trigger the display of related job openings. Job seekers will also receive career and labor market information that is relevant to their job search.

In addition to the services provided, the centers also have resource rooms where customers can find local, state and national job vacancy listings in both electronic and paper form. Computers are available for use and are equipped with word processing software to write resumes and letters to employers. They are equipped with career information delivery systems which enable the user to locate more information about the world of work and the opportunities available. The resource rooms frequently contain a career library with books, videos, and software on a variety of employment topics. Many states include telephones, fax machines, photocopiers and Internet connections in resource rooms. These rooms sometimes contain video conference facilities which allow for long-distance job interviews. The centers have amassed a number of tools that will improve a potential worker's opportunity for success in the job market.

The staff in the one-stop career centers provide individual and group career assessment and counseling. They offer training in a wide variety of job search skills such as resume preparation, completing an application, interviewing, networking, and effectively using the telephone. They also facilitate job clubs or groups on topics of interest to those seeking employment (Mariani 1997).

The Department of Labor began implementing the initiative by awarding planning and implementation grants to states. The grants were intended to be used for the cost of system building. Since the startup, planning grants have been awarded to all states. The federal government has given the states flexibility in the design of their systems. There are however, four basic requirements:

1. *Universality*. All state residents must be given access to a menu of the following basic services: information on careers, occupational demand and wages, and the availability and quality of education and training programs; test and assessment; information on job openings and hiring requirements; job referrals; assistance with job search skills; eligibility information on programs and services available within the community.

2. *Customer Choice*. Individuals and employers must be given a choice as to how they will obtain the information, basic services, and education and training programs that they need. In addition, they must be given sufficient qualitative information about training and education options so that they can make an informed choice.

3. *Integration*. Programs, services and governance structures for the following programs must be integrated and accessible through the one-stop system: dislocated worker programs;

employment service programs; veterans employment service programs; JTPA Title II training programs for adults; senior community service employment programs; and unemployment insurance. In addition, the Department of Labor encourages and gives preference in awarding grants to systems that include other Department of Labor funded programs including migrant and seasonal farm worker programs, Job Corps, school-to-work initiatives, food stamp, employment and training, welfare-to-work training programs, adult education, vocational rehabilitation, postsecondary programs funded under the Vocational Education Act, and federal/state student financial aid programs.

4. *Performance-Driven Outcome-Based.* Each state must establish outcome measures that will be used to evaluate the system and hold it accountable for both performance and service to users.

(Boetz 1997)

How are states meeting these four requirements? Many states have invested in technology, including the development of software and the technology infrastructure needed to meet both consumer and employer needs. Many states are developing automated systems that consumers can access through the Internet. Once on the Internet they can obtain information about available job openings, career options, local and state employers, and labor markets. Information about the range and quality of education and training services is also included in the systems. Many offices also have their own Web sites. Some also use public access or college television stations to broadcast training programs, scroll job listings on screen, or announce events scheduled at the centers (Mariani 1997). In rural areas, one-stop offices are staffed by a smaller number of people but have the full range of services available electronically. In some states, these services are delivered by a mobile staff that move from one office to another.

A number of states are working on access through technology that will allow for self-assessment of basic skills and occupational skills/interests, instruction in basic skills or job search techniques, and skills certification. The goal is to balance automation with personal service.

ONE STATE'S APPROACH

Wisconsin has 78 one-stop career centers throughout the state. Services are provided in either a self-, lite, or intensive service track depending on the needs of the job seeker and the employer.

- Level 1. Self-service is intended to be used with little or no assistance from staff. Examples include access to information on job openings, careers, employment training programs, employment support services, and community resources.
- Level 2. Lite service is intended to be used by job seekers and employers with limited interaction with the staff. Interaction can be in the form of brief one-on-one assistance or more lengthy participation in group activities. Examples include assessment activities, job seekers workshops, and assistance with employment search and career exploration.
- Level 3. Individualized or specialized service is intended to be used by those who need intensive levels of service over an extended period of time. This level of service is generally provided through a staff person with an "individual service plan." Examples include individual financial and employment planning, case management, employment support services, participation in short- and long-term employment training programs, and enrollment in educational programs. Services in this category are often targeted by federal and state law.

In Wisconsin, a location can qualify as a center if it has the following services available: area-wide interagency planning, intake, assessment, case management, employer relations, and services provided on site.

At a minimum, the partners at the center need to include a job service, the local technical college, local private industry council, vocational rehabilitation services, and the W-2 welfare reform agency. Additional partners might include community action programs, economic development agencies, apprenticeship councils, literacy agencies, organized labor, and other community-based organizations.

In Wisconsin, as elsewhere, the one-stop approach helps customers who are confused about which program will meet their
needs. This approach also helps disseminate information to those
who are unaware of available services. Working together, the agencies eliminate duplication of effort and wasted resources, increase
awareness of the services available, join forces to meet the unique
needs of all their customers, increase the efficiency and effectiveness of their programs, and make the best use of public tax dollars.

Typical services in a Wisconsin center might include

- specific and individual job training, retraining and career
  guidance;
- JobNet automated self-service job matching system;
- complete and accessible labor market information;
- vocational rehabilitation;
- vocational education and training;
- entry-level and re-entry counseling;
- resume-writing assistance;
- job search workshops and interviewing clinics;
- individualized skills assessment;
- aptitude testing;
- individualized job search and employment planning;
- job search-related financial counseling and assistance; and
- job related transportation and child care information.

A TOOL FOR SERVICE DELIVERY
A portfolio is a tool that provides adults with a step-by-step
approach to planning a career, making decisions, and putting
together an action plan that will help them reach their goals. The
portfolio also helps adults

- learn more about themselves in terms of how they relate
  to the world of work;
- guide themselves through the steps of career planning;
- create a place to record information about past, current,
  and future work; and
- store and organize important career and work-related
  information.

The particular portfolio discussed in this example is *Creating Your Life's Work* (from JIST Works, Inc., 720 North Park Avenue, Indianapolis, IN 46202-3490). There are five sections in this particular portfolio.

- Section 1. *Information on Who I Am.* The activities help adults gather information to better understand who they are and how they operate. They spend time examining their skills, abilities, life roles, and discover how they grow and change.
- Section 2. *What I Can Do.* The next section of the portfolio looks at the skills an individual can offer a prospective employer. These same experiences, skills, and accomplishments are clues that can help direct an individual to future occupations. This section helps an individual choose an occupation, put a resume together, fill out job applications, and prepare for interviews.
- Section 3. *Exploring Career Options.* Next comes an analysis of the work world. This section leads an individual through the exploration of occupations and the labor market. It also looks at how skills and abilities relate to the world of work.
- Section 4. *Deciding on a Career Direction.* To make decisions about a career, it helps to have a system for making those decisions. This section gives the user a step-by-step model for making career decisions.
- Section 5. *Getting and Keeping Your Job.* In the last section the individual is guided through the steps needed to plan for landing a job in their career area of interest. There is also information in this section about keeping a job.

Whether individuals are beginning their careers or have years of experience, this portfolio takes them through a step-by-step career planning process. This type of portfolio helps clients to both create a place (the portfolio) and a process for career development. It is one comprehensive way to help the adults who come into the one-stop career centers.

Summary

Adults face career issues and concerns that differ from those of young people, specifically

- lack of awareness of the wide range of occupations available to them,
- lack of direction,
- not having kept up with changes in the world of work,
- having a single career orientation,
- lack of understanding of the pros and cons of changing careers,
- feeling of unfulfillment in their present situation, and
- looking for challenge and meaning in their career.

With this in mind, adult career development centers must focus on

- self-knowledge,
- information on the workplace and work environment, and
- a system for obtaining and integrating this information: creating an action plan.

In 1994, the U.S. Department of Labor introduced the concept of the one-stop career center. While providing the services listed above, these centers bring together publicly funded employment and training services in one place. One-stop career centers may also include private initiatives such as the United Way, and generally take advantage of Internet technology to reach clients away from the physical career center itself.

Chapter 10

Planning for Action

by Don Schutt

This action plan is intended to serve as a road map for the processes described in the preceding chapters. Any good planning process recognizes that three factors often determine success. First, it is necessary to set goals to achieve goals. Second, writing goals down and reviewing them often increases the chances of meeting those goals. Finally, if the goals involve groups of people (a group defined here simply as more than one person), it is important to have a level of agreement within the group relative to the goals. Goal setting is sometimes viewed as an arduous task because it is important to not only build into the plan the strategies for evaluation, but also to adhere to that plan. Recognizing growth and progress toward goals can reinvigorate, decrease the burden that evaluation seems to be, and offer an opportunity for reflection and, one hopes, celebration, as the career center succeeds.

This chapter discusses preplanning activities as well as action planning. The level of detail in this action plan has been minimized so that a broader planning picture surfaces. Each of the components of the action plan have been discussed in the planning and development chapters or demonstrated in the chapters depicting career centers in action.

Preplanning Activities

Identify who will initially lead the development of the career center

- ✔ Choose an individual or group capable of succeeding in developing the career center.
- ✔ Identify a person or a group with

- a working knowledge of career development;
- the authority or access to the authority necessary to make decisions;
- collaborative relationships with key potential partners;
- the capability to effectively and efficiently facilitate a task-oriented work group through the completion of a large-scale project;
- the creativity necessary to navigate complex challenges;
- access to relevant individual, community, or organizational information; and
- the respect of those in the community or organization.

Set the Stage

✔ Build the career center on a sound conceptual foundation comprising
  - clear career-related definitions;
  - understandable, user-friendly processes (answering the three questions);
  - access for all potential users;
  - resources to broaden or reinforce users' self-knowledge and understanding;
  - strategies to increase individual users' capacity for managing virtually limitless information; and
  - an endorsement for the inclusion of education, work, family, cultural, and economic factors/issues in lifelong personal career development plans.

✔ Recognize that the ultimate goal of the career center activities is to empower individuals to become the architects of their career development.

✔ As an organization, embrace and advocate for the subtle yet significant shift from a transition or placement focus to an individual lifelong career development focus. If the career center is intended to be transition- or placement-focused (as some might), be sure to identify to users the specific role in the career development process that your center is addressing with support and services.

Action Planning

Step One: Define Concerns, Challenges, and Needs

✔ Plan a needs assessment that identifies both individual and community needs—the goal is to compare what is already in existence with what needs to be provided.
- Collect data to substantiate or challenge previous findings or assumptions.
- Identify individual, organizational, and community needs, concerns, and challenges.
- Determine why this is a concern, challenge, or need.

✔ Determine what other information is needed to make a good decision when addressing this challenge.

✔ Prioritize the issues by importance, if possible; you might find that some concerns are symptomatic of a more intense challenge.

✔ Translate to goals (or more broadly into mission or purpose).

Step Two: Seek Solutions

✔ Review the goals.
- Address the goals with the easiest solutions.
- Identify the challenges demanding more complex solutions.
- Re-evaluate the priorities.

✔ Identify indicators of success.
- Define measures of success gathered through formative evaluation.
- Similarly, define measures of overall programmatic (summative) success.

✔ Determine what will prevent you from succeeding.
- Respond with creative solutions to obstacles.
- Re-evaluate the obstacles relative to the importance of the goal.

✔ Connect solutions to resources (including staff and materials).
- Choose an advisory group.
- Plan for recruiting and hiring staff.

- Identify resources.
- Assessment tools.
- Career and labor market information.
- Strategy-based references.
- Create a plan for choosing a location.

✔ Develop a budget connected to resources that are in turn connected to solutions.

Step Three: Implement the Action Plan

✔ Identify time frames.

✔ Establish your career center as an entity.
- Recruit and hire staff.
- Evaluate materials.
- Develop a plan for organizing and maintaining resources.
- Choose a permanent location.
- Select a design and layout for the center.
- Locate necessary equipment.
- Consider how to respond to new and emerging technology.
- Market to appropriate constituencies.

✔ Enlist supporters/partners to increase visibility or collaborate in delivering services (with help from the advisory group).

✔ Communicate with key elements of your public.

✔ Practice continuous planning and improvement.
- Engage in continuous discussion to develop or review mission, purpose, and roles.
- Create a plan for integrating/infusing evaluation findings into practice.

✔ Ask regularly: "What are the concerns/challenges/needs of the population we serve?" This, of course, returns you to Step One.

Summary

Career centers can serve as the hub around which career development occurs in any given environment. They capture the hopes and dreams along with the realities of the interplay between education and work, work and leisure, and family culture and work. Many of the people in today's workforce got into their current positions through hard work, low to moderate levels of planning, and happenstance. While these courses of action may have been useful, there is little doubt that to succeed in today's workforce, a more thoughtful and organized approach can add to one's success whether that success is measured in a new, different or better job or in greater satisfaction in one's current employment.

It is important to carefully examine the conceptual foundation that guides the development of the career center, and to recognize (and then publicize) the role of the center in the career development processes of individuals. Further, identifying individual needs and then providing developmentally appropriate support, services, and activities is a cornerstone of effective practice.

While a magic formula for creating a career center would be ideal, no such formula exists. Success results from your capacity to take these suggestions and recommendations, translate them into useful processes and systems that are sensitive to the demands within your environment, and combine them with your unique community resources to meet the needs of your audience. The prerequisite for taking such action is planning for action.

Chapter 11

Career Centers Online

by Don Schutt

Career centers take a number of different forms on the Internet. Virtual career centers, by definition, exist only on the Internet. This is the case for many of the centers that offer services online, but it is also the case that existing career centers in physical locations are developing Web interfaces to extend their services well beyond their geographic and time limitations. This provides exciting opportunities for connecting career center users with vital and bountiful information on the Internet, but it should be approached with caution. As the number of Websites offering career development assistance increases, so does the possibility that users will be mislead, misinformed, or charged for services that may be neither comprehensive nor useful. Accepting both the positive and negative possibilities, this chapter considers the development, implementation, and management of an online career center. Several sites that deliver career-related information and services are also highlighted.

At one point in time, locating and accessing career and labor market information was the primary challenge facing those considering their career development. The Internet is proving to be a useful solution to that problem; now, the challenge has become synthesizing the plethora of information into a manageable and personally meaningful career plan. Sampson (1997) proposed that the Internet could serve four specific functions for its users:

1. "Identify problems and possibilities by using links to surf among Internet sites to discover the range of data that is available, e.g., surfing serendipity.
2. Search for information to solve a problem by using a search engine or an Internet site.

3. Obtain information when users know what they want by accessing a specific Internet site or by using a search engine to link to a specific Internet site address.
4. Communicate with others via email, file transfer, chat mode, and eventually videoconferencing."

The Internet is used in many different ways to deliver career development. Some Websites serve specific populations such as the American Chemical Society's (ACS) employment resources site (http://www.acs.org/careers.empres/workforc.htm). ACS, concerned about the number of traditional jobs in chemistry, delivers an excerpt of an article on the Web page to assist chemists seeking employment outside of science. It discusses broad topics like "the changing nature of work" and "traditional versus nontraditional work" as well as more specific topics such as "resumes and interviews" and "resources to research employers."

Other sites serve as clearinghouses for additional sites. Two examples are the California Career and Employment Center's "Useful Links" page (http://www.webcom.com/~career/links.html), and the "Catapult on JOBWEB" supported by the National Association of Colleges and Employers (http://www.jobweb.org/catapult/catapult.htm). The Catapult provides links to other sites, resources for career practitioners, help guides and library resources, and professional development opportunities.

With so much information and so many sites, how can the Internet be used effectively for career development? Sampson (1997) suggested that the Internet should not be used in isolation from other career development resources, but in conjunction with them. Similarly, it is important to combine Internet use with periods of reflection and of interaction with others. Sampson (1997) also suggested that the Internet be used primarily for networking and gathering information, while bearing in mind that users must be directed to the Websites that are most appropriate for their individual needs.

Further consideration has been given to the delivery of career information and planning services as well as Webcounseling services. The National Career Development Association addressed these issues in the "Guidelines for the Use of the Internet for Provision of Career Information and Planning Services" (http://ncda.org/polweb.html). Similarly, the National Board for Certified Counselors, Inc. has also developed "Standards for the Ethical Practice of WebCounseling" (http://www.nbcc.org/wcstandards.htm).

Planning a Website

When planning a Website, there are some basic questions that need to be addressed:

- What is your purpose?
- Who are you trying to reach?
- Who are your competitors and how will you differ from them?
- What resources do you have for set-up and maintenance?
- What are your expectations of success?
- How will you measure success?

(Based on Tauber and Kienan 1997)

These questions are similar to questions asked in the planning stages for physical career centers. The most important step is deciding on a clear purpose for the site and developing the structure and content on paper prior to putting the Website together. Often, sites are developed "on-the-fly" and lack consistent graphical themes, send users in information loops that never end, and ultimately lose users due to poor planning. To prevent this from occurring, create a flow chart that follows each step a user would experience as they move about your site.

In deciding how Web pages should be arranged, it is best to aim for something between the extremes of a dull, book-like format and an overwhelming excess of graphics and hypermedia. The first approach clearly does not take proper advantage of hyperlinks and similar features that make Internet use so quick, easy, and enjoyable. The second approach has the unpleasant effect of showing off exciting features at the expense of simple navigation and even of substantial information. Two examples of organizational techniques that can be employed include a hierarchical approach and multiple tracks for multiple audiences. The hierarchical approach follows an outline with the ability to build as many levels as needed. If the pages are accessed by individuals with different levels of experience in either the content or the process, it may be worthwhile to consider a multiple path approach.

The CareerInfoNet Website exemplifies the multiple path approach for different audiences. Developed as a cooperative effort by educational institutions, businesses, and government, it provides students and job seekers in the community of West Bend and Washington County, Wisconsin, with an integrated and dynamic source of electronic information about career information and opportunities. Users are able to access the site from one of the official locations including middle schools, high schools, colleges, public libraries, and the local workforce development center or from any computer with an Internet connection. The career information on the site is drawn from local, state, and national sources and is continually updated.

The home page for CareerInfoNet is: http://www.careernet.org/. To officially enter the site, users are asked to complete an online registration form (http://www.careernet.org/register.htm). The registration form gathers background information and provides a glimpse into the multiple paths by asking if the user is a parent or a student. The main menu of the site includes lifework planning (in which the multiple paths are embedded) along with a number of other pages including information and resources available to use in the decision making process (http://www.careernet.org/mainmenu.htm). By choosing "Life-work Planning," the planning paths for students, parents, counselors, teachers, and employers (as well as other resources) become visible (http://www.careernet.org/plan/index.htm). To sample the multiple paths, choose two of the options paths and compare. As an example, "Teacher" was chosen (http://www.careernet.org/plan/teacher.htm). The "Teacher" page provides activities along with links to other informational pages like an opportunity to visit the lifework planning process information page.

When planning the center's Website, consider these tips from Tauber and Kienan (1997) for creating smashing Web pages:

- Give your site a title that's brief, descriptive, and easy to remember.
- Keep the title's promise, and provide all content you say you will.
- At the top of each page, offer clues about what's on the page. Don't assume that people are going to scroll unless you give them a reason to scroll. Break pages that are more than three screenfuls long into multiple pages.
- Make anything that looks like a button act like a button.
- Make links meaningful—avoid generic "Click Here" links, and decide whether you're going to link on the active phrase ("Go To") or the destination phrase ("Our Chat Archive").
- Use small image files that contain no more than 50 colors.
- Keep directory names and filenames short and consistent.
- Tell your users the size of any downloadable files—they need to know whether they can manage a file of this size.
- Provide an email link to the Webmaster.
- Before you announce the site, test it until you can't stand to test it anymore. Get others to test it. Find all the bugs and squash them. Then launch.

Managing the Online Career Center

One of the most fundamental choices in regard to managing the online career center is whether you will host the site yourself or use an Internet service provider (ISP). If the former, you must thoroughly research the amount of resources—time, money, staff—involved in such a task, as these can be considerable. If the latter, you must still make provision for paying and interfacing with the ISP. Your university, school district, or company may already have Internet services or connections that you can take advantage of, so it is best to examine this possibility before taking any action.

Staffing

Staffing the Web presence is an important task that often requires many different individuals. Internet-related job titles can be confusing and job descriptions often change with the technology, but most Websites require workers in the following roles: Webmasters, Web developers, network systems administrators, programmers, and customer service representatives. A career center hosting its own large site might require more than one person in each role, whereas smaller sites might have just one or two people filling all of these positions. A career center using an ISP may only have a part-time Webmaster on staff to communicate ideas, changes, and problems to the ISP.

Briefly, the *Webmaster* is, as the term implies, the authority on what goes into the Website, when it goes in, how it will look, and all the other concerns of starting and maintaining the site. Nevertheless, the Webmaster of a university or corporation Website, for example, may ultimately have to answer to a higher authority such as a dean or vice president. Tauber and Kienan (1997) described four types of Webmasters: the tech Webmaster with hardcore technical skills, the content Webmaster well-versed in creating content, the production Webmaster handling everything from design to scanning art, and the executive Webmaster with perhaps no Web experience but plenty of project management expertise.

Web developers (also called *designers* or *publishers*) are "responsible for the actual creation of the Website. After collaborating with the Webmaster to lay out the conceptual framework of the site and establish performance constraints, the developer begins the day-to-day activities necessary to design the Web pages" (Steinberg 1997).

Network systems administrators keep the network's computers up and running. Responsible for facilitating the links between servers and Internet providers, they might also monitor network traffic.

Programmers essentially implement the ideas of Webmasters or Web developers, though they may be one and the same person. They write instructions for computers using Hypertext Markup Language (HTML), which tells browsers how to display each page. Programmers frequently customize existing or off-the-shelf software to meet specific needs.

Customer service representatives offer business or technical support, usually on behalf of Internet service providers. Only those career centers hosting their own sites are likely to have customer service representatives, but these representatives often provide necessary assistance when a site is not operating properly.

The Website Budget

Consider three different expense classes when developing Website budgets: infrastructure, production, and ongoing support. Again, there will be appreciable differences between budgets for career centers hosting their own sites and those that use ISPs. *Infrastructure* encompasses all of the tangible items needed to construct and maintain a site, from office space and computers to an Internet connection and related telephone bills. *Production* costs include everything involved in getting the site up and running, such as design and programming expenses. *Ongoing support* usually involves paying people to regularly update the site or add new materials to it as needed. It can be tempting to cut costs by reducing this part of the budget, but Websites lose their attraction and usefulness if they are not kept up to date. If you are unwilling or unable to maintain the site as you should, it might be best to reevaluate your plans to go online.

Measuring Success

Planning for evaluation is as important for Websites as it is for other aspects of the career center. Often, measuring success on the Internet is a challenging endeavor for many reasons. One is that defining success is difficult enough without the complicating factor of technology. Another is that technology factor itself: what information is gathered and how that indicates success. The following summary provides suggestions for measuring the success of Web pages:

- Hits, impressions, and traffic reports: Hits are the number of files that are accessed on your Website. A hit is generated for every page of text and every graphic or video file. A single page may generate a number of hits. Impressions occur each time a single page on your site is loaded. It is a much better indicator of popularity but more difficult to measure. Traffic counts the number of visits that have occurred in a discrete time frame. The challenge in counting traffic is deciding how to measure it. If you can figure that part out, you can gather valuable data about your Web use.
- Media presence: How much media attention do you receive? Even a mention in the local paper can indicate that your site is generating interest. Another method of measuring the popularity of your site is to count the backlinks—or the links on other sites that go to your site.
- Information gathered and reported: Perhaps understanding the center's target population more thoroughly is success in itself. You can gather data while also gaining an understanding of how popular your site is.
- Subject responses: If users mention the site, perhaps in responses to the Webmaster from the email prompt, consider this subjective data as useful as other measures of success.

(Condensed from Tauber and Kienan 1997)

Examples

There are a number of career center sites worth visiting on the Internet to sample a variety of methods of delivering career information.

- ALMIS State Occupational Projections: http://udesc.state.ut.us/almis/stateproj/
- America's Job Bank featuring search tips along with job market information, employers and job seekers sites, and job market information: http://www.ajb.dni.us/
- Career Mosaic with jobs, employers, an online job fair and career network: http://www.careermosaic.com/cm/home.html

- Florida State University Career Center providing services for a number of different groups: http://www.fsu.edu/~career/
- Monster Board Career Center with Resume Builder, career resources, career advice, relocating services, and other links: http://www.monster.com/pf/careerc/center.htm
- Online Career Center with a search function and recruiting office.

One challenge facing career centers attempting to provide career services on the Internet is how to teach the process of career development and then support that process. Most of the sites listed here (and in the majority of career-related Internet books) offer pieces that support the career development process but do not teach or support the whole process. That process, once again, consists of answering three questions: Who am I?, Where am I going?, and How do I get there? Many of the career-related sites are helpful to users making a transition from one situation to another, but few of the sites focus on a lifelong process of developing career maturity and making lifelong, personally meaningful plans.

There is one notable exception that is moving in the direction necessary to provide more comprehensive career planning and development services on the Internet. Connected to Bowling Green State University (http://www.cba.bgsu.edu/class/webclass/nagye/career/process.html), this site is quite simply titled the "Career Planning Process." The site provides basic information on the process of career development along with some helpful beginning activities and information. The challenge is providing the expertise necessary to guide an individual through the career development process. While this site offers a different approach than the great majority of sites, more work needs to be done before it can replicate the expertise available at a material career center.

Summary

Career centers on the Internet may serve a variety of purposes and users, including

- replicating the services of a physical career center for those unable to reach it,
- supplementing the basic services of a physical career center,
- assisting only a specific population (i.e., medical students, displaced workers),
- acting as a clearinghouse for other career-related sites, and
- actually taking the place of a physical career center.

Planning a Web Page

Before you write a single line of HTML, take time to consider and answer completely the following questions:

- What is your purpose (perhaps one of those listed above)?
- Who are you trying to reach?
- Who are your competitors and how will you differ from them?
- What resources do you have for set-up and maintenance?
- What are your expectations of success?
- How will you measure success?

As you proceed with your online career center, bear in mind that the medium of the Internet has its pitfalls as well as exciting possibilities. While accessing masses of job listings or blithely following link after link, users can easily be distracted from the entire process of career development. With careful planning and informed usage, however, career centers online can be a worthwhile and innovative addition to the career development process.

Chapter 12

What Does the Future Hold?

by Carl McDaniels

In the future, it may be convenient to point to a computer and say: "That is our career center! Everything you need is in there." But what a mistake that would be! Career centers for the future need a far more thoughtful and comprehensive approach than that. They should be multidimensional to accommodate their users' many different learning styles. They should reflect the modern world of work and the modern approach to preparing for it and living in it.

This chapter suggests some, but not necessarily all, of the signposts that will guide career centers in the future. These are meant to be suggestions for most settings and will probably trigger other ideas as local needs dictate. The one point that *all* career centers need to consider, now as well as in the future, is the need to be user-friendly. This is implied in the ten signposts below as well as in the eleven previous chapters. After the very best career center is planned and developed, it is only effective if people use it to the fullest possible extent. There has to be a major ongoing effort to make centers attractive, inviting, comfortable, bright, accessible, relevant, and—most importantly—helpful to a variety of target populations.

Ten Signposts for Career Centers of the Future

1. Firsthand Experience is the Best Source of Career Information

The best source of career information has always been personal experience. It may now be called *experiential learning* or *hands-on learning,* but it still means getting out and learning about education and employment firsthand. For example, it has always been better to visit a college for a few days when classes are in session than to read about it in a brochure. It is infinitely better to see, feel, and smell the campus than to take a virtual tour on its Website. Likewise, the best way to judge continuing education efforts is to visit a class instead of reading a course description. It's not always possible to arrange firsthand experiences, but it is always best to make the effort. A key element in an effective and comprehensive career center for the future is full-scale arrangements for affective learning in addition to cognitive learning; this is where the center's connections to the local community pay off. Career centers can arrange or direct users toward

- part-time work opportunities, both long- and short-term;
- summer employment, possibly as replacements for vacationing workers;
- volunteer opportunities in local, state, or national programs;
- service learning experiences;
- occupational and educational information interviewing;
- job shadowing experiences;
- cooperative work-study opportunities;
- internships;
- ongoing relationships with occupational mentors and role models;
- visits to institutions of higher learning; and
- summer camp experiences on college campuses.

2. A Multimedia Approach

Just as in today's libraries, tomorrow's career centers must accommodate a variety of learning styles. Some users who are not computer literate may feel more comfortable taking home a magazine or newspaper featuring vocational information. Others may choose to watch a video rather than to read a book, or they may want to call a career information hotline to speak directly to a professional. The point is simple and obvious: the career center that takes a one-dimensional approach to disseminating information will serve only a very limited number and narrow band of clients. That may be acceptable in a facility serving only college graduates, for example, who are all highly literate and computer literate as well. More often, however, career centers must deal with users who have varying reading levels and technological competence. To ensure a true multimedia approach, career centers should aim for the following kinds of resources:

- Print materials such as occupational and educational newspapers (general and specialized), magazines, brochures, books, pamphlets, reprints, monographs, and briefs
- Large visuals including posters and pictures on all aspects of users' career development such as financial aid, apprenticeships, state licensed occupations, fastest growing career fields, local training options, and accredited home study programs
- Audio and video tapes on an appropriate range of career topics for the target user groups
- Access to appropriate computer software and Internet access to at least one local, state, regional, or national career information delivery system (CIDS)
- Career information telephone hotlines, ideally linked to another career center, a CIDS, or similar source

3. Serving Diverse Users, Especially Women, Minorities, and Persons with Disabling Conditions of *All* Age Levels

Obviously, other specific groups such as veterans, retirees, and those who speak English as a second language could also be highlighted here. The point is that the diversity of users must be given thoughtful consideration in the career center of the future. Each center will have to determine the best way to do this given the particulars of its own situation, but here are three general suggestions.

1. Provide access to mentors and role models from the groups mentioned above who can personally relate to the users' problems and concerns. In recent pre-employment activities with persons moving from welfare-to-work, two things made the greatest impact: a) Role models formerly on welfare but now successful wage earners, family members,

and lifelong learners; and b) Mentors who were there on a continuing basis for comfort, understanding, and encouragement.

2. Provide print materials and software that speak to diverse groups. Make a special effort to show that the modern world of work is open to all.

3. Take advantage of the latest technology to assist users with special needs. Ready access to TDD and TTY phone connections are as necessary as books in Braille and other special assistive devices. Specialized software and Web sites are increasingly becoming available for the user groups mentioned here.

4. The Changing Workplace: Flextime, Flexplace, Flexpay, Job Sharing, Part-Time, and Temporary Work

Full-time, long-term employment with a single company is no longer the ideal it once was—yet many career centers and professionals are unprepared to deal with that. People are often astonished to learn that Manpower—the temporary hiring firm—employs more people than any other company in the United States. This firm, along with Kelly Services, Accutemps, and hundreds of other temping firms around the country, should be presented as real options for adults seeking less than regular full-time employment. Job sharing and part-time jobs also deserve consideration.

Likewise, information about flexible working arrangements needs to be a part of career centers in the future. Such arrangements may be made at the convenience of the employee or the employer—or, in the best of circumstances, at the convenience of both. Flextime may involve working a shift, say 9:00 AM to 3:00 PM, that allows a parent to be at home whenever school-age children are. Flexplace may provide work-at-home (or telecommuting) options. In any case, there are more and more options beyond the traditional workweek that can interest career center users for a variety of family, educational, personal, or financial reasons.

The Three Wild Cards

The next trio of signposts have been called the "three wild cards" in the workplace of the twenty-first century. These three are often ignored by career centers showcasing only large, traditional employers—but career centers of the future will need to feature small business, entrepreneur, and work-at-home options.

5. Small Business Opportunities

Many of the fastest-growing employment opportunities across the United States are in small businesses. Most often defined as employers with fewer than 500 employees, small businesses are more likely to have only 25 to 100 employees. For the most part, they are firms less than 25 years old, often involved in health care technology or service-related fields. Beyond the famous success stories of Microsoft, Dell, and Gateway computers, there are hundreds of successful small businesses in almost every career field, from publishing to landscaping. Career centers need to feature opportunities in small business just as much as large corporations or multinational firms.

One major aspect of small business that career centers can easily feature is that of franchises. Many of the small employers in most communities are franchise operations, such as:

- Fast food: Burger King, Hardees, McDonald's, Wendy's
- Gasoline: Exxon, Mobile, Shell, Texaco
- Auto dealers: Chrysler, Ford, GM, Honda, Subaru
- Motels: Comfort Inn, Days Inn, Hampton Inn, Holiday Inn
- Pizza: Domino's, Little Caesar's, Pizza Hut
- Miscellaneous: Budget Rent-a-Car; Jiffy Lube; Mail Boxes, Etc.

To properly feature small business opportunities, it is important to have the latest magazines—*Inc., Success, Franchise*—books, software, access to Web sites, and other information on the important area of future employment. A great resource in this area is the Small Business Association, which can be reached at 800-827-5722 or on the Web at http://www.sba.gov

6. Entrepreneurship

One of the dominant forces in the economy of the next century (and the source of much of its job growth) will be entrepreneurship. This usually involves innovative ideas characterized by uncertainty and risk, complementary managerial competencies, and creative opportunism. These factors distinguish entrepreneurship from other small business or work-at-home opportunities. Bringing this concept to career center users may mean locating examples of successful entrepreneurs as well as illustrations of how products and services can be targeted toward unfulfilled niche markets—such as the ones filled by Michael Dell with Dell Computers and Debbie Fields with Mrs. Fields' Cookies. A further reason to feature entrepreneurship in career centers is the great promise this area offers for women, minorities, and people with disabling conditions. Community contacts and various multimedia resources—including *Black Enterprise, Entrepreneur,* and *Venture*—can help career centers of the future emphasize this exciting career option.

7. Work-at-Home Opportunities

Although no exact figures are available, Bell South estimates that over 30 million people work at home. Other estimates range between 20 and 25 million, which are still formidable numbers—and a good reason for including information about this important area of work in the career center of the future. Work-at-home simply refers to people who work out of their apartments, houses, farms, etc. Some people who work at home are self-employed. There are four general categories of work-at-home self-employment:

1. Traditional: accountant, cosmetologist, insurance salesperson, photographer
2. Direct Sales: Amway, Avon, Fuller Brush, Mary Kay, Tupperware
3. Craft: calligrapher, leather-worker, potter, quilter
4. Miscellaneous: bed and breakfast, catering, cleaning, consulting

Other people who work at home are employed by outside firms, doing such work as sales, writing, or data entry. Some people combine this kind of work with self-employment.

With such large numbers of people involved in work-at-home and every indication that their numbers will continue to grow, career centers must begin to present information on this as a career option. Resources in this area are somewhat difficult to find, but there are some good small newsletters and magazines such as *Solo, National Home Business Report, Home Business Magazine,* and a variety of books. Again, the career center's connections to the local community can really pay off here by connecting its clients with mentors and role models from the work-at-home sector.

8. Serving Older Adults

Demographics strongly suggest that the career center of the future will need to serve older adults, the most rapidly growing segment of the American population. Right now, roughly one-third of the population is 45 years of age or older and, because of the aging of the baby boom generation, that percentage is growing faster than any other age group. For the most part, this group is mobile and can afford many of the educational opportunities now open to them on a full- or part-time basis. For many, this means the chance to complete a degree begun years ago or to pursue an interest in art, drama, landscaping, or computers that was not practical or even available when they were last in school. There are now many opportunities open only to people over 55 years of age, such as Elderhostels. Elderhostel sponsors one- to three-week learning programs across the United States, Canada, and more than 70 foreign countries; more information is available from them at 75 Federal Street, Boston, MA 02110-1941 or on their Website at http://www.elderhostel.org

In addition to educational information for older adults, occupational information—especially that related to the three wild cards listed above—is very important. For the older adult who wants to work at home, this may be the perfect time to try to turn a hobby into a lucrative business. Speaking of hobbies, since the older population is living longer and staying healthier, the career center that serves this population is advised to provide up-to-date information on leisure activities as well. The interaction between leisure and work is much more apparent to older adults than to younger people, particularly when the definition of leisure includes physical, social, intellectual, volunteer, and creative activities.

9. Serving Low-Income and Unemployed Persons

One of the biggest challenges of the future from a career development standpoint is how to improve career center services for low-income and unemployed clients. The most obvious illustration of this is the nationwide effort called *welfare-to-work* or *welfare reform*. As of late 1998, some 3 million former welfare recipients are working full- or part-time or combining education and work. This group needs career center services both as a part of the pre-employment process (prior to beginning work or school) and after they have begun working at a minimum wage job and realized that the way up is through more training and education. This may, in fact, prove the largest and most significant role that career centers play in the next five to ten or even twenty years as welfare reform sends increasing numbers of people to them for help. Similar groups in search of services will include those workers displaced by downsizing, mergers, or closures who have some skills but need additional training and guidance to re-enter the workforce.

Special consideration must be given to the resources needed by this growing user group. Reading levels and attractiveness are especially important. The creation of "mini-career centers" in libraries, community centers, and welfare offices may be worth trying. More personal assistance may be necessary for people who have been out of work or disconnected from education for a number of years. The availability of mentors and role models through career centers may be the most important resource of all. The one-stop career centers now sponsored by the U.S. Department of Labor will serve some of this large user group, but not all. Career centers in every community will have to be prepared to serve them.

10. Self-Directed Assessment

Frank Parsons, the "father of vocational guidance," emphasized in his 1909 book *Choosing a Vocation* three broad factors in what we now call career development: understand yourself, understand the world of work, and engage in true reasoning based on these two groups of facts. The first part of this process has often been misunderstood or overlooked in favor of the "test 'em and tell 'em" method: give young people a test and it will reveal who they are and what they should be. In the future, there should be renewed consideration of Parsons' notion of self-discovery and self-understanding by way of a *process* of self-directed assessment. Such a process would ideally include one or more of the firsthand experiences mentioned at signpost one, which give clients an idea of their strengths and weaknesses as well as their likes and dislikes.

Self-directed assessment is beginning to attract attention now, so there is a growing number of self-assessment instruments on the market. Some are improved interest inventories, others help make the connection between leisure interests and work possibilities. Add to these the growing interest in portfolio development (discussed in Chapter Four, Critical Center Resources) and it becomes evident that career centers will have the tools they need to make self-directed assessment one of their services.

Finally, Never Be Satisfied

Two recent studies underscore the reason career centers should never be satisfied. The first is the American Council on Education's *Too Little Knowledge is a Dangerous Thing: What the Public Thinks and Knows about Paying for College.* The study found that most adults have no clue as to how much a college education costs, where students can find financial aid, and just how much aid is available. The authors commented that "the public continues to grossly overestimate the price of going to college and many believe that it is unaffordable for a majority of families." Specifically, the study found that parents overestimated the cost of tuition by three times the accurate amount! The second study, by ACT, revealed that 42 percent of high school seniors who took the ACT exam said they needed more assistance with educational and occupational planning—and very small percentages were selecting majors in computer and information science or computer engineering, the occupations with the highest projected growth over the next decade. Clearly, these two studies demonstrate that today's college freshman and their parents are badly in need of accurate, up-to-date, timely, and usable career information—the kind that should be readily available in every career center.

A key point in all of these signposts is that the quality career center for the future should always be a work-in-progress. Career centers should always be thought of as being under construction, never completed, never good enough. There must always be new ideas and methods under consideration, old resources under review. It has been suggested that career centers keep nothing over five years old except perhaps for a section of "golden oldies"—time-honored resources offering solid, enduring ideas.

And, as has been noted throughout this book, the career center for the future must engage in constant evaluation as part of never being satisfied. This means that everyone who uses the center must have input in its direction, along with focus groups and advisory boards. There are always better ways to provide assistance through personal service and expanded resources. There are always more convenient hours and more accessible floorplans for the center to try. There is always new and changing technology to consider and evaluate. There are always new and better local resources waiting to be incorporated into the career center's services. Ultimately, all career centers for the future need to fit cognitive and affective information together into a delivery system or process that is constantly under review and improvement for the optimum career development of each user.

Bibliography

Bagin, D., Gallagher, D. R., and Kindred, L. W. 1994. *The school and community relations.* 5th ed. Needham Heights, MA: Allyn and Bacon.

Barbieri, M. 1991. *Career resource center handbook.* Commerce, TX: East Texas State University, Commerce, Educational Development and Training Center.

Boetz, B. 1997. *Surfing the tsunami.* Washington, DC: American Counseling Association.

Borchard, D. C. 1995. Planning for career and life: Job surfing on the tidal waves of change. *The Futurist* 29(1): 8-12.

Bridges, W. 1994. *Job shift: How to prosper in a workplace without jobs.* Menlo Park, CA: Addison-Wesley Publishing Co.

Brown, D., and Brooks, L. 1991. *Career counseling techniques.* Boston: Allyn and Bacon.

Brown, D., and Brooks, L. 1996. *Career choice and development.* 3d ed. San Francisco: Jossey-Bass Publishers.

Brown, S. T., and Brown, D. 1990. *Designing and implementing a career information center.* Garret Park, MD: National Career Development Association.

Caffarella, R. S. 1994. *Planning programs for adult learners: A practical guide for educators, trainers, and staff developers.* San Francisco: Jossey-Bass Publishers.

Casella, D. A. 1990. Career networking: The newest career center paradigm. *Journal of Career Planning and Employment* 50(4): 32-39.

Celente, G. 1997. *Trends 2000.* New York: Warner Books.

Center on Education and Work, University of Wisconsin-Madison. 1996. *Wisconsin career centers pilot study: Final report.* Madison, WI: Center on Education and Work, University of Wisconsin-Madison.

Collard, B. A., Waterman, J., and Waterman, R. 1994. Toward a career-resilient work force. *Harvard Business Review* July/August: 87–95.

Department of Workforce Development, Division of Connecting Education and Work. 1997. *Wisconsin career centers: An information guide.* Madison, WI: Department of Workforce Development, Division of Connecting Education and Work.

DeYoung, L. 1998. *Do it: Career development series: Career and labor market information.* Madison, WI: Center on Education and Work, University of Wisconsin-Madison.

Engels, D. W., ed. 1994. *The professional practice of career counseling and consultation: A resource document.* 2d ed. Alexandria, VA: National Career Development Association.

Ettinger, J. M. 1996a. *Improved career decision making in a changing world: Participant's resource guide.* 2d ed. Garrett Park, MD: Garrett Park Press.

Ettinger, J. M. 1996b. *Improved career decision making in a changing world: Training manual.* 2d ed. Garrett Park, MD: Garrett Park Press.

Florida State University, Tallahassee, Center for Instructional Development and Services. 1990. *Establishing and operating a career resource center. A bibliography.* Tallahassee, FL: Florida State Department of Education, Division of Vocational, Adult, and Community Education.

Golden, B. 1997. Does your technology deliver? *Techniques: Making Education and Career Connections* 72(7): 16-19.

Guthrie, B., Maxwell, S., Mosier, P., Nadaskay, P., and Vallejos, M. 1990. *A career center handbook for New Mexico's high school counselors.* Alamogordo, NM: New Mexico State University.

Gutteridge, T. G., Leibowitz, Z. B., and Shore, J. E. 1993. *Organizational career development: Benchmarks for building a world-class workforce.* San Francisco: Jossey-Bass Publishers.

Gysbers, N. C. 1996. Beyond career development—Life career development revisited. In *Career transitions in turbulent times: Exploring work, learning and careers,* ed. R. Feller and G. R. Walz. Greensboro, NC: ERIC/CASS Publications.

Gysbers, N. C., and Henderson, P. 1994. *Developing and managing your school guidance program.* 2d ed. Alexandria, VA: American Counseling Association.

Hall, D. T., ed. 1996. *The career is dead—Long live the career.* San Francisco: Jossey-Bass Publishers.

Hansen, L. S. 1997. *Integrative life planning: Critical tasks for career development and changing life patterns.* San Francisco: Jossey-Bass Publishers.

Herr, E. L., and Cramer, S. H. 1996. *Career guidance and counseling through the life span: Systematic approaches.* 5th ed. New York: HarperCollins.

Hispanic Dropout Project. 1998. *No more excuses: The final report of the Hispanic Dropout Project.* Madison, WI: Hispanic Dropout Project.

Hoffinger, A., and Goldberg, C. 1995. *Connecting activities in school-to-career programs: A user's manual.* Boston: Bay State Skills Corporation.

Hoppin, J. 1994. *Workforce in Transition.* Washington, DC: National Occupational Information Coordinating Committee.

Isaac, S., and Michael, W. B. 1984. *Handbook in research and evaluation.* San Diego: EDITS Publishers.

Jandt, F., and Nemnich, M. 1997. *Using the Internet and the World Wide Web in your job search: The complete guide to online job seeking and career information.* Indianapolis. IN: JIST Works.

Kapes, J. T., and Vacha-Haase, T. 1994a. Additional career assessment instruments. Chapter 15 in *A counselor's guide to career assessment instruments,* ed. J. T. Kapes, M. M. Mastie, and E. A. Whitfield. 3d ed. Alexandria, VA: National Career Development Association.

Kapes, J. T., and Vacha-Haase, T. 1994b. A counselor's guide users' matrix: An alphabetical listing of career assessment instruments by category and type of use. In *A counselor's guide to career assessment instruments,* ed. J. T. Kapes, M. M. Mastie, and E. A. Whitfield. 3d ed. Alexandria, VA: National Career Development Association.

Kapes, J. T., Mastie, M. M., and Whitfield, E. A. 1994. Introduction to *A counselor's guide to career assessment instruments.* 3d ed. Alexandria, VA: National Career Development Association.

Kennedy, M. M. 1997. Has time become the new currency? *Kennedy Career Strategist* 12(8): 3-4.

Knowles, M. 1978. *The adult learner: A neglected species.* 2nd ed. Houston, TX: Gulf Publishing Co.

Kobylarz, L., ed. 1996. *National career development guidelines: Trainer's manual.* Washington, DC: National Occupational Information Coordinating Committee.

Leiken, E. 1996. The Net: Where it's @. *Techniques: Making Education and Career Connections* 71(8): 34-40.

Mariani, M. 1997. One-stop career centers: All in one place and everyplace. *Occupational Outlook Quarterly*: 3-15

Marshall, B. 1982. *Career resource centers: Overview: ERIC fact sheet no. 7.* Washington, DC: National Institute of Education.

McDaniels, C., and Gysbers, N. C. 1992. *Counseling for career development: Theories, resources, and practice.* San Francisco: Jossey-Bass Publishers.

Mehrens, W. A. 1994. Selecting a career assessment instrument. Chapter 3 in *A counselor's guide to career assessment instruments,* ed. J. T. Kapes, M. M. Mastie, and E. A. Whitfield. 3d ed. Alexandria, VA: National Career Development Association.

Myers, K. A. 1998. Letter to editor, 9 March.

National Career Development Association (NCDA). 1994. *Career literature, software, and video review guidelines.* Alexandria, VA: NCDA.

National Occupational Information Coordinating Committee (NOICC). 1989. *The national career development guidelines: Trainer's manual.* Washington, DC: NOICC.

National Occupational Information Coordinating Committee (NOICC). 1995. *Program guide: Planning to meet career development needs: School-to-work transition programs.* 2d ed. Washington, DC: NOICC.

National Occupational Information Coordinating Committee (NOICC). 1997. *Life work portfolio.* Indianapolis, IN: JIST Works.

National Organization for Women (NOW). 1972. *Women on words and images.* Washington, DC: NOW.

Parsons, F. 1909. *Choosing a vocation.* Boston: Houghton Mifflin.

Ramey, L., and Splete, H. 1995. *Adult career counseling center: Twelfth annual report, September 1994–June 1995.* Rochester, MI: Oakland University.

Rayman, J. R. 1996. Apples and oranges in the career center: Reaction to R. Reardon. *Journal of Counseling and Development* 74(3): 286-287.

Ross, B. 1995. *Lasting gifts: Parents, teens and the career journey.* Edmonton, AB: Alberta Advanced Education and Career Development.

Rothwell, W. J., and Kazanas, H. C. 1992. *Mastering the instructional design process: A systematic approach.* San Francisco: Jossey-Bass Publishers.

Saltzman, A. 1991. *Downshifting: Reinventing success at a slower track.* New York: Harper Collins.

Sampson, J. P., Jr. 1997. The Internet as a potent force for social change. In *Social action: A mandate for counselors,* ed. C. C. Lee and G. R. Walz. Greensboro, NC: ERIC/CASS Publications.

Sampson, J. P., Jr., Kolodinsky, R., and Greeno, B. 1997. Counseling on the information highway: Future possibilities and potential problems. *Journal of Counseling and Development* 75: 203-212.

Schilling, D., Schwallie-Giddis, P., and Giddis, W. J. 1995. *Preparing teens for the world of work: A school-to-work transition guide for counselors, teachers and career specialists.* Spring Valley, CA: Innerchoice Publishing.

Schmidt, A., and de Wolf, C. 1997. *Final report: Wisconsin career centers: A study of three centers.* Madison, WI: Center on Education and Work, University of Wisconsin-Madison.

Schutt, D. A. 1996. *Implementing a vision: The creation of a school-community career center.* Presentation to CESA Organization, 10 October, in Portage, WI.

Schutt, D. A., Brittingham, K. V., Perrone, P. A., Bilzing, D., and Thompson, M. J. 1997. *The Wisconsin developmental guidance model: A resource and planning guide for school-community teams.* Madison, WI: Wisconsin Department of Public Instruction.

Secretary's Commission on Achieving Necessary Skills. 1992. *Learning and living: A blueprint for high performance—A*

SCANS report for America 2000. Washington, DC: Secretary's Commission on Achieving Necessary Skills.

Steinberg, G. 1997. Jobs associated with the Internet. *Occupational Outlook Quarterly* 41 (2): 2-9.

Tauber, D. A. and Kienan, B. 1997. *Webmastering for dummies.* Foster City, CA: IDG Books Worldwide.

Taylor, D. 1997. *Creating cool Web pages with HTML.* 3d ed. Foster City, CA: IDG Books Worldwide.

Tennessee State Department of Education. 1990. *Comprehensive career development project: career center guide.* Nashville, TN: Tennessee State Department of Education.

Tindall, L. W., Gugerty, J. J., Thuli, K. J., Phelps, B. R., and Stoddard, D. 1994. *Ideas to help you solve your ADA problems.* Madison, WI: Center on Education and Work, University of Wisconsin-Madison.

Tittell, E., and James, S. N. 1997. *HTML for dummies.* 3d ed. Foster City, CA: IDG Books Worldwide.

Wagner, J. O. 1993. *Career resource centers.* Greensboro, NC: ERIC/CASS Publications.

Weddle, P. D. 1995. *Electronic resumes for the new job market.* Manassas Park, VA: Impact Publications.

Wessel, R. D. 1998. Career centers and career development professionals of the 1990s. *Journal of Career Development* 24(3): 163-177.

Worthen, B. R., and Sanders, J. R. 1987. *Educational evaluation: Alternative approaches and practical guidelines.* White Plains, NY: Longman.

Zalinsky. 1993. ERIC Document ED362808.

Zunker, V. G. 1981. *Career counseling: Applied concepts of life planning.* Monterey, CA: Brooks/Cole Publishing Co.

State Occupational Information Coordinating Committees

Alabama OICC
Center for Commerce, Rm. 424
401 Adams Ave., PO Box 5690
Montgomery, AL 36103-5690
Tel: 334-242-2990
Homepage: http://soiccal.huntingdon.edu/SOICC/default.ow

Alaska OICC
Dept. of Labor, Research & Analysis
PO Box 25501
Juneau, AK 99802
Tel: 907-465-4518

Arizona OICC
1789 W. Jefferson, 1st Fl.
PO Box 6123, Site Code 897J
Phoenix, AZ 85005-6123
Tel: 602-542-3871

Arkansas OICC
Div. of Employment Security
Employment & Training Services, PO Box 2981
Little Rock, AR 72203
Tel: 501-682-3159

California OICC
660 J St., Rm. 400
PO Box 1138
Sacramento, CA 95812-1138
Tel: 916-323-6544
Homepage: http://www.soicc.ca.gov/

Colorado OICC
1515 Arapahoe St.
Tower Two, Level 3, Suite 300
Denver, CO 80202-2117

Tel: 303-620-4981
Homepage: http://www.cosoicc.org/

Connecticut OICC

Dept. of Labor
200 Folly Brook Blvd.
Wethersfield, CT 06109-1114
Tel: 860-566-5368
Homepage: http://www.ctdol.state.ct.us/soicc/soicc.htm

Delaware OICC

Office of Occup. & LMI, Dept. of Labor
University Office Plaza, PO Box 9965
Wilmington, DE 19809-0965
Tel: 302-761-8050
Homepage: http://www.oolmi.net/

District of Columbia OICC

500 C St., N.W. Suite. 201
Washington, DC 20001
Tel: 202-724-7631

Florida OICC

Hartman Bldg., Suite 200
2012 Capital Circle, S.E.
Tallahassee, FL 32399-2151
Tel: 850-488-1048
Homepage: http://lmi.floridajobs.org/

Georgia OICC

Dept. of Labor, 148 International Blvd.
Sussex Place
Atlanta, GA 30303
Tel: 404-656-9639
Homepage: http://www.dol.state.ga.us/lmi

Hawaii OICC

830 Punchbowl St., Rm. 321
Honolulu, HI 96813
Tel: 808-586-8750
Homepage: http://www.pixi.com/~hsoicc/

Idaho OICC

Len B. Jordan Bldg., Rm. 301
650 W. State St., PO Box 83720
Boise, ID 83720-0095
Tel: 208-334-3705

Homepage: http://www.sde.state.id.us/cis/cishome.htm

Illinois OICC
217 E. Monroe, Suite 203
Springfield, IL 62706
Tel: 217-785-0789
Homepage: http://www.ioicc.state.il.us/

Indiana OICC
Dept. of Workforce Development & Technical Education
10 N. Senate Ave, Rm. SE212
Indianapolis, IN 46204-2277
Tel: 317-233-5099
Homepage: http://www.dwd.state.in.us/

Iowa OICC
Workforce Development
1000 E. Grand Ave.
Des Moines, IA 50319
Tel: 515-242-5032
Homepage: http://www.state.ia.us/iwd/isoicc

Kansas OICC
119 Grant St.
Chanute, KS 66720
Tel: 316-431-4950

Kentucky OICC
500 Mero St., Rm. 2031
Frankfort, KY 40601
Tel: 502-564-4258

Louisiana OICC
PO Box 94094
Baton Rouge, LA 70804-9094
Tel: 504-342-5151

Maine OICC
Bureau of Employment Services
55 State House Station
Augusta, ME 04333-0055
Tel: 207-624-6390

Maryland OICC
Dept. of Labor, Licensing & Regulation
1100 North Eutaw St., Rm. 203
Baltimore, MD 21201

Tel: 410-767-2953
Homepage: http://www.careernet.state.md.us./MOICC.htm

Massachusetts OICC
Government Center, Div. of ES
C.F. Hurley Bldg., 2nd Fl.
Boston, MA 02114
Tel: 617-626-5718

Michigan OICC
Victor Office Center, 4th Fl.
201 N. Washington Sq.
Lansing, MI 48913
Tel: 517-373-0363

Minnesota OICC
Dept. of Econ. Security
390 N. Robert St.
St. Paul, MN 55101
Tel: 651-296-2072
Homepage: http://www.des.state.mn.us/lmi/careers

Mississippi OICC
301 W. Pearl St.
Jackson, MS 39203-3089
Tel: 601-949-2240

Missouri OICC
400 Dix Rd.
Jefferson City, MO 65109
Tel: 573-751-3800
Homepage: http://www.works.state.mo.us/moicc

Montana OICC
1301 Lockey St., 2nd Fl., PO Box 1728
Helena, MT 59624-1728
Tel: 406-444-2741
Homepage: http://jsd.dli.mt.gov/lmi/mcis.htm

Nebraska OICC
550 S. 16th St.
Lincoln, NE 68509-4600
Tel: 402-471-9964
Homepage: http://www.dol.state.ne.us

Nevada OICC
Research & Analysis, DETR

500 E. Third St.
Carson City, NV 89713-0021
Tel: 702-687-4550

New Hampshire OICC
64 Old Suncook Rd.
Concord, NH 03301
Tel: 603-228-3349
Homepage: http://www.state.nh.us/soiccnh

New Jersey OICC
PO Box 057, 5th Fl.
Trenton, NJ 08625-0057
Tel: 609-292-2682
Homepage: http://wnjpin.state.nj.us/OneStopCareerCenter/SOICC/

New Mexico OICC
401 Broadway, N.E., Tiwa Bldg.
PO Box 1928
Albuquerque, NM 87103
Tel: 505-841-8455
Homepage: http://www3.state.nm.us/dol/soicc.htm

New York OICC
Dept. of Labor, Research & Statistics
State Campus, Bldg. 12, Rm. 488
Albany, NY 12240
Tel: 518-457-3806

North Carolina OICC
700 Wade Ave., PO Box 25903
Raleigh, NC 27611
Tel: 919-733-6700
Homepage: http://www.esc.state.nc.us/soicc/

North Dakota OICC
1720 Burnt Boat Dr., PO Box 5507
Bismarck, ND 58506-5507
Tel: 701-328-9734
Homepage: http://www.state.nd.us/jsnd/soicc.htm

Ohio OICC
Div. of LMI, Bureau of Employment Services
145 S. Front St.
Columbus, OH 43215
Tel: 614-466-1109
Homepage: http://www.ohio.gov/lmi

Oklahoma OICC

Dept. of Vo-Tech Education
1500 W. 7th Ave.
Stillwater, OK 74074
Tel: 405-743-5198
Homepage: http://www.okvotech.org/soicc/index.htm

Oregon OICC

875 Union St., N.E.
Salem, OR 97311
Tel: 503-947-1233
Homepage: http://olmis.emp.state.or.us

Pennsylvania OICC

Research & Statistics
220 Labor & Industry Bldg, 7th & Forster
Harrisburg, PA 17121-0001
Tel: 717-787-6466

Rhode Island OICC

101 Friendship St.
Providence, RI 02903
Tel: 401-272-0830
Homepage: http://www.det.state.ri.us/webdev/lmi/rioicchm.html

South Carolina OICC

631 Hampton St., PO Box 995
Columbia, SC 29202
Tel: 803-737-2733
Homepage: http://www.scois.org

South Dakota OICC

DOL, 420 S. Roosevelt St.
PO Box 4730
Aberdeen, SD 57402-4730
Tel: 605-626-2314

Tennessee OICC

11th Fl., Volunteer Plaza
500 James Robertson Pkwy.
Nashville, TN 37245-1600
Tel: 615-741-6451

Texas OICC

Whitney Jordan Plaza
9001 IH-35 North, Suite 103-B
Austin, TX 78753-5233

Tel: 512-491-4941
Homepage: http://www.soicc.state.tx.us

Utah OICC
Dept. of ES, PO Box 45249
140 East 300 South
Salt Lake City, UT 84147
Tel: 801-536-7806

Vermont OICC
5 Green Mountain Dr., PO Box 488
Montpelier, VT 05602
Tel: 802-828-4394
Homepage: http://www.det.state.vt.us/

Virginia OICC
Employ. Comm.
703 E. Main St., PO Box 1358
Richmond, VA 23211
Tel: 804-786-7496

Washington OICC
Dept. of Employment Security, PO Box 9046
Olympia, WA 98507-9046
Tel: 360-438-4803
Homepage: http://www.wa.gov/esd/lmea/soicc/sohome.htm

West Virginia OICC
PO Box 487
Institute, WV 25112-0487
Tel: 304-599-8318
Homepage: http://www.wvsoicc.org

Wisconsin OICC
Dept. of Workforce Dev., PO Box 7944
201 E. Washington Ave., GEF-1, Rm. 221X
Madison, WI 53707-7944
Tel: 608-267-9611
Homepage: http://www.dwd.state.wi.us/dwelmi/

Wyoming OICC
246 S. Center St., 2nd Fl.
PO Box 2760
Casper, WY 82602
Tel: 307-473-3809

Index